WAYMARK

RED · GUIDE

KENT

MICHAEL McNAY

The orchards form a great feature of the country; and the plantations of Ashes and of Chestnuts . . . add greatly to the beauty . . .

WILLIAM COBBETT, *Rural Rides*

RED GUIDE
KENT

MICHAEL McNAY

FOR SUE

AUTHOR
Michael McNay

ILLUSTRATOR
Mark Peppé

ADDITIONAL RESEARCH
Peter Wenham; John Vigar

COVER ILLUSTRATION
Glyn Dawson

EDITING
First Edition

TOWN INFORMATION PANELS
Vijay Patel; additional work by Virginia Langer

CARTOGRAPHY
© *The Automobile Association 1989*

Typeset by
Avonset, Midsomer Norton, Bath

Printed and bound by
Richard Clay Limited, Bungay,
Suffolk

The contents of this publication
are believed correct at the time of
printing. Nevertheless, the
Publishers cannot accept
responsibility for errors or
omissions, nor for changes in
details given.

Published by
Waymark Publications,
an imprint of The
Automobile Association

© The Automobile Association 1989

All rights reserved.
No part of this publication may
be reproduced, stored in a
retrieval system or transmitted
in any form or by any means –
electronic, mechanical,
photocopying, recording or
otherwise – unless the written
permission of the copyright
owner has been given
beforehand

Produced and distributed in the
United Kingdom by the
Publishing Division of
The Automobile Association,
Fanum House, Basingstoke,
Hampshire RG21 2EA

ISBN 0 86145 809 5

HOW TO USE THIS BOOK

The *Red Guide Kent* divides the county into five sections. These sections are divided again into smaller areas to explore. Most of the smaller areas begin with a description of the largest town, or another good place to start a tour. This is followed by an exploration of the surrounding area.

The map on pages 6–7 shows starting points for local tours, with page numbers.

A complete, alphabetical list of all the places in the book is given in the index at the end of the book, together with details of other books on the county.

Town information panels
Practical information is given for selected towns. This includes early closing and market days, cashpoints, tourist information centres, places to visit, leisure centres, cinemas, and access by road and rail. Places to visit which are closed for much of the year, or which only open on a few days of the week are marked *. At the time of going to press, places not marked with an asterisk were open all year round, and on most days of the week. Tourist information centres will have details of any changes.

For information on places mentioned elsewhere in the book, contact local tourist information offices, or the regional tourist board:
South East England Tourist Board, 1 Warwick Park, Tunbridge Wells, Kent TN2 5TA.

Or see The Automobile Association's annual guide to places to visit in Britain.

Other useful addresses:
English Heritage, 23 Savile Row, London W1X 2BT

Kent Trust for Nature Conservation, The Annexe, 1a Bower Mount Road, Maidstone , Kent ME16 8AX

National Trust, 36 Queen Anne's Gate, London SW1H 9AS

National Gardens Scheme (private gardens opened occasionally to the public), 57 Lower Belgrave Street, London SW1W 0LR. Annual booklet available in shops in spring.

Royal Society for Protection of Birds (RSPB), The Lodge, Sandy, Beds SG19 2DL

Royal Society for Nature Conservation (RSNC), The Green, Nettleham, Lincoln LN2 2NR

CONTENTS

INTRODUCTION

FROM THE END of the pier, with your back to the Downs and dark clouds scudding overhead, it is easy to see Deal as J M W Turner saw it when he painted the watercolour that hangs in the old town hall. Some things have changed. Most of the buildings on the beach side of the front have been demolished. But the Royal Hotel, built in the reign of George II, is still there, flag stretched taut from the top of the flagpole. And by the sea, as far back as the High Street, the town is a maze of eighteenth-century shops, cottages, and pubs, with one or two grander houses among them.

Look again. Imagine the shoreline without houses: that is how Julius Caesar saw the coast of Kent in 55BC when, seeing the armed Belgae ranged on the cliffs of Dover, he had second thoughts about landing there and sailed around the South Foreland to the first level strand he could find. Then, and in his second exploration the following year, Caesar's stays were short and warlike; even so, he saw enough to write the first description of Kent's topography. Kent, he said, was a purely maritime district (the forested Weald of the interior was almost impassable). Most ships from the Continent made their landing on the east coast and Kent's inhabitants, being the closest to Gaul, were by far the most civilised.

The Emperor Claudius invaded a hundred years after Julius Caesar. He laid down the first infrastructure of roads, and almost every development since then has hung from the framework of that great Roman endeavour.

One great difference is the changed shape of the coast, which radically altered the fortunes of ports such as Sandwich, Tenterden and New Romney. Otherwise, looking below the surface layers, the Romans might recognise Kent from the broad geographical sweep to the intimate detail of field patterns. First there is the marshy hinterland of the Thames, rising slowly to the North Downs whose chalk scarp slope stretches from Hampshire into Kent at Westerham and right through to Dover. Beneath the downs is the wooded slope of the greensand, then the Weald, and Romney Marsh. Within its confines, some 60 miles east to west, fewer than 40 north to south, Kent has vast panoramas of woodland and pasture, small intimate valleys, bleak stretches of marshland, orchards and hop gardens, wide fields of wheat, market gardens.

Its landscape has at one time or another sustained fishing, coal mining, iron manufacture, ship building, brick making, cement works; and with the Thames as the northern border and Kent's own great river, the Medway, navigable for miles beyond Maidstone, water was once at the heart of the county's economy. Parish registers deep in the heart of Kent record the life's passage of hoymen and sailmakers, recalling the days when roads were impassable and timber and crops, bricks and iron were transported to the port of Rochester and beyond, to London, to Essex and to the Continent, by boat.

But any exploration of Kent can only start in one place:

. . . from every shire's end
In England, down to Canterbury
* they wend*
To seek the holy blissful martyr . . .

MICHAEL McNAY

Christopher Marlowe
Born in Canterbury, Marlowe was by any standards a great poet; his *Tamurlane the Great, Dr Faustus,* and *Edward II* are second only in Elizabethan and Jacobean drama to Shakespeare's plays. Yet the traffic through Deptford passes by St Nicholas's parish church where Marlowe lies buried in obscurity, and all Kent can show is a theatre in his birthplace named after the playwright.

Christopher Marlowe was born in 1564, the son of a shoemaker, and educated at King's School and Corpus Christi, Cambridge. Soon after, he left for London. *Tamurlane* (1590) was his first play; its metrical experiments introduced a new flexibility and expressiveness into English dramatic verse. He seems to have known Shakespeare and was a friend of Sir Francis Walsingham, who lived at Scadbury, a moated house near Chislehurst (its remains can still be seen). Walsingham was Queen Elizabeth II's Secretary of State and employed Marlowe as a spy. Marlowe's atheistical views were unpopular with authority and he was on the run from the law on this issue when he was stabbed to death in a public house in Deptford in what was described as a drunken brawl. The church register is inscribed: 'Christopher Marlowe, slain by ffrancis Archer 1 June 1593'. He was barely 29.

1 Canterbury, the Stour Valley and Thanet

When Reginald Fitzurse, Hugh de Moreville, William de Tracy and Richard le Breton unsheathed their swords in the north transept of Canterbury Cathedral and cut down Archbishop Becket they ensured the prosperity of the city and church for the next 350 years, until King Henry VIII broke with the Pope. Then, with Becket's glittering shrine in the Trinity Chapel destroyed, Canterbury became a backwater and its archbishops increasingly and at last exclusively spent their time at Lambeth, not even coming to Kent for their enthronement. So nowadays a revived Canterbury is probably more like the medieval city than it is like the town Defoe described in the 18th century as 'a general ruin a little recovered': Chaucer's pilgrims would certainly recognise the bustle of today's Canterbury.

CANTERBURY
Canterbury, roughly, follows a cruciform plan. The streets of the Roman city of Durovernum were overlaid by Saxon and medieval building; and the city to see is the city of Chaucer and of Canterbury's native son, Marlowe. The centrepiece is the cathedral, described at length further on. Starting outside the cathedral at the gorgeous 15th-century Christ Church Gate and moving up Mercery Lane to the High Street, the building on the right-hand corner with the pronounced jetty overhanging the street was the medieval Chequers of the Hope, part of the huge pilgrim inn of Chaucer's day. Here, the right arm of the cross leads over the Stour to the ancient West Gate and up the hill beyond the city wall to St Dunstan's. This was the parish church of the Roper family, and it is here that Margaret Roper, Sir Thomas More's daughter, brought his head after his execution

and had it buried. Along the way is the cherishable Queen Elizabeth's guest chamber, 17th-century and richly pargeted with highly coloured putti flying among swags of grapes. Then the egregiously over-ornate 19th-century Royal Museum and Art Gallery and the much admired (and much restored) weaver's cottages of 1561 beside the Stour (and other cottages equally picturesque down All Saints Alley), where Huguenot weavers worked after fleeing France when Louis revoked the Edict of Nantes in 1685. Almost opposite is the Eastbridge Hospital, founded about the time of the death of Becket and dedicated to him. It has a contemporary undercroft and in the hall up a short flight of steps a 12th-century painting of Christ in Glory, in a mandorla surrounded by the evangelists (though only two have survived). Near at hand, down Stour Street, are other fine medieval buildings: the Greyfriars, the surviving building of a Franciscan friary founded soon after St Francis's death in the 13th century, and the Poor Priests' Hospital.

The left arm of the cross leads through the part of the city that suffered worst in the bombing and the rebuilding, out through the walls and on to the ruins of St Augustine's Abbey. It was contemporary with the cathedral and survived until the Reformation in 1540. It has unquestionable archaeological and deep historical interest. For me, however, the short walk up the hill to St Martin's is much more rewarding. After the departure of the Romans and the invasions of Saxons and Jutes, pockets of Christianity remained. When Augustine arrived to fulfil Pope Gregory I's commission to convert the heathen, he found a king, Ethelbert, married to a Christian queen, Bertha. The Venerable Bede tells us in his history of England (written less than a century and a half later), that 'on the east side of the city stood an old church, built in honour of Saint Martin

Canterbury

Population: 36,507

Market Days: Wed, Sat

Cashpoints: *Barclays* 6 Rose Lane; *Lloyds* 49 High St; *Midland* 1 The Parade, Whitefriars – Gravel Walk; *Nat West* 11 The Parade, Longmarket – 7 George's St

Tourist Information: 34, St Margarets St (or Herne Bay)

Attractions: Canterbury Cathedral, Canterbury Heritage, Canterbury Pilgrims' Way, Roman Mosaic Pavement, Royal Museum and Art Gallery and Buffs Regimental Museum, St Augustine's Abbey, West Gate Museum

Arts: Canterbury Centre (St Alfreds Centre), Gulbenkian Theatre, Marlowe Theatre

Leisure: Kingsmead Road Swimming Pool

Cinema: Cannon Cinema

By Road: London 61 miles (A2, M2), Maidstone 27 miles (A2, M2, A249), Dover 16 miles (A2)

By Rail: 1hr 20mins from London (London, Victoria to Dover line – Canterbury East Station). Direct services from Canterbury West to Ramsgate and Ashford. Direct services from Canterbury East to Dover and Chatham

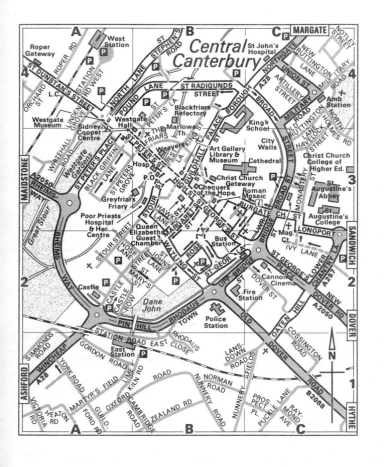

Canterbury

during the Roman occupation of Britain, where the Christian queen of whom I have spoken went to pray.' There are at least half a dozen churches in Kent which incorporate Roman brick into their structures, but at St Martin's great stretches of wall, especially on the south of the chancel, are Roman. There is no reason to doubt that this little parish church looking down across St Augustine's (and Canterbury Jail) to the cathedral, is where Augustine and his followers assembled with Queen Bertha 'to sing the psalms, to pray, to say Mass, to preach, and to baptise, until the king's own conversion to the faith gave them greater freedom to preach and to build and restore churches everywhere'. Perhaps it needs a stretch of the imagination to picture St Augustine, Queen Bertha and a newly converted King Ethelbert, but precisely because St Martin's is still a church, still a place of christenings and weddings (with a simple Norman font of real grandeur), the effort is easily made.

Weavers' cottages, Canterbury

Go back to the city along the main road, Longport, and then turn left to take a walk along the city wall, over Queningate, reputedly Queen Bertha's way to and from St Martin's, and along beside the beautifully laid out and maintained gardens below (on one side; on the other a busy ring road and scenes of commerce and industry). This is Dane John garden, with a path winding up a tall prehistoric tumulus crowned by an 19th-century monument. Here the city walls, 14th-century with Roman foundations, which run right round from north of the cathedral, come to an end at the castle, now a ruined keep merely.

The road leading from the castle back to Mercery Lane (the southern arm of the cross) is lined with Tudor and Georgian houses.

North of the cathedral, the last arm of the cross goes along Palace Street and St Radigund's Street among several other churches and the old Dominican friary, the Blackfriars, set in a lovely garden, to a crossing of the Stour at the Causeway where a little pub, the Miller's Arms, makes Canterbury Ales in one of the smallest breweries in England.

One other shrine remains in Canterbury. Along the Old Dover Road is St Lawrence's ground, where Kent County Cricket Club has its headquarters. Go there on an ordinary Monday during a county championship match, and enjoy the hallucination that England, our England, has never changed.

Within the blessed circle of trees, things have changed since the days of the legendary 19th-century all-rounder, Fuller Pilch, but not so that it matters. Cars are parked among the horse chestnuts, boots open, tablecloths spread on picnic tables loaded with smoked salmon and cold roast chicken, and corks pop. The pavilion with its clock on a little white gable is flanked by newer grandstands, named for famous Kentish cricketers – the great wicket keeper Leslie Ames and the batsman Frank Woolley – but these names are drowned out by advertising hoardings, covering every spare vertical surface. Around the eastern boundary is a range of marquees erected by sponsors to entertain clients. The batsman at the crease brings up his 50 with an elegant cut past the lime tree standing just inside the third-man boundary to a restrained round of applause from the spectators.

Canterbury Cathedral

Part of the cathedral's personality is unquestionably its Englishness, typically seen from Herbert Baker's War Memorial garden under the city wall planted with masses of flowers. Crucially it is the height of the great tower that holds together the cathedral composition, balancing out the great length of nave, choir, retrochoir (here known as the Trinity Chapel) and Corona (the easternmost end). Bell Harry, the Angel steeple, vies with

Greyfriars and Blackfriars
St Francis of Assisi and St Dominic were contemporaries. St Francis founded his order of friars in 1209, St Dominic in 1215. By 1224 a group of Franciscans, or greyfriars, had already settled in Canterbury. In 1267 they were granted a new site, and the lovely Greyfriars building straddling the Stour dates from them. The Dominicans, or Blackfriars, arrived in England in 1221 and their prior immediately impressed Archbishop Langton with his preaching. So although it was not until 1237 under a new Archbishop that the Dominicans settled in Canterbury the ground was prepared. They were made welcome by the Archbishop and the monks of Christ Church and Henry III granted them the riverside land where the Blackfriars still stands. He and his successors continued to lavish gifts upon the blackfriars and by their own energy they enclosed more land and erected more buildings. Unlike the blackfriars, the greyfriars were a mendicant order; dedicated, that is, to poverty. They were forbidden to own property (Greyfriars was rented to them), but still managed to accumulate a valuable library, many of whose volumes are now in the British Library. Two friars, Richard Risby and Hugh Rich, had the misfortune to be supporters of the Holy Maid of Kent (see page 126) and were executed with her at Tyburn. The king dissolved both friaries in 1538.

Becket's Martyrdom
In hindsight the martyrdom of Thomas Becket was one of history's great inevitable tragedies. Becket had been Henry II's friend and chancellor and was trained in the church by Henry's first archbishop, Theobald. As chancellor, Becket seems to have been a worldly, sophisticated figure. He was renowned for his entertainments and celebrated as a diplomat and a soldier. After he had been appointed archbishop in 1162, however, he showed a far more austere side and fought fiercely for the rights of the church. He excommunicated people who had appropriated church lands, and resisted the King's moves to have clergy tried in secular courts. The king undermined Becket's position by offering the insult of having his son, Henry the Younger, crowned king (to establish his inheritance ahead of time) by the Archbishop of York. Becket excommunicated York. Henry, who was in France, responded with the ill-starred exclamation (or something very similar): 'Will no one rid me of this turbulent priest?' The Bishop of Rouen rebuked him gently for his intemperance and the matter was forgotten; except that four knights slipped out of the assembly, rode hard to the Channel, crossed on a favourable wind, slept the night at Saltwood, and on a dark 29 December 1170 cut Becket down in Canterbury Cathedral.

with Durham's great crossing tower as the noblest in England, and yet it is extraordinarily elegant in the detail of the decoration of its façade and the filigree finesse of its pinnacles.

Bell Harry was finished in 1504, the last major work at Canterbury Cathedral and separated from the building of Anselm's Romanesque tower adjacent to it by as long a period as the centuries that separate us from Bell Harry's building. Purists complain that Canterbury is not a stylistic unity. But of all great churches Canterbury most successfully combines the styles of centuries: here a Decorated window piercing a Norman wall; there Anselm's Norman stair tower adjacent to Wastell's late Perpendicular crossing tower, and the Perpendicular nave leading to the early Gothic choir, Trinity Chapel, and Corona.

You enter the cathedral through the south-west porch, whose empty niches for sculpture were filled in 1857 with figures from Canterbury's past, like King Ethelbert, Queen Bertha and St Augustine. The sculptor was a Belgian called Thomas Pfyffers. He received £24 for each figure, money which was not well spent.

The nave is, simply, wonderful. Not even the simplicity of Yevele's other great nave, at Westminster Abbey, is preparation for this. The nave followed the line of the exterior walls built by the first Norman archbishop, Lanfranc. The floor of the north transept, hallowed by Becket's blood, could not be touched. So Yevele built narrowly, and he built high and clear and untrammelled, with slender, soaring piers instead of the mighty bulk of the Romanesque. Yet by one of those strokes of Gothic magic, the gaze embraces not just the nave, but the whole sweep of the church. In most cathedrals the screen interrupts the view. At Canterbury, too, there is a stone screen in front of the choir at the top of a majestic flight of steps. But there is a central entrance

1 Nave
2 South Aisle
3 South Transept
4 St Michael's Chapel
5 The Crossing – beneath Bell Harry Tower
6 Choir
7 Tomb of the Black Prince
8 St Anselm's Chapel
9 Trinity Chapel – site of Becket's Shrine
10 Corona
11 Site of Becket's Martyrdom
12 The Crypt: Chapel of Our
   Lady of the Undercroft.

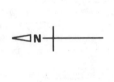

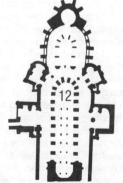

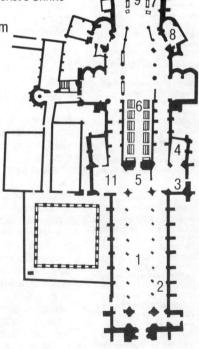

Henry Yevele

The myth of the Gothic craftsman grafting away in holy anonymity dies hard, but Canterbury Cathedral gives it the lie. Here, records survive, and so do the names: William of Sens, who built the choir, and William the Englishman, who added the Trinity Chapel and Corona, John Wastell, who built the loveliest crossing tower in Christendom, Thomas Mapilton, Richard Beke, Stephen Lote, and others. Best-known of them all was Henry Yevele, not just because he built the naves both at Canterbury and at Westminster Abbey, but because he was, at a shilling a day, director of the king's works at Westminster and at the Tower. That meant he could 'impress' – or pressgang – others in the building trade, and had the power to imprison any who refused to serve.

A lot of his work in London is still identifiable; Canterbury apart, this is not so in Kent, but he is known to have worked in Rochester, repairing both the bridge and the castle; and evidence suggests that he was also master mason or architect of Cooling Castle. Local tradition has it that he at least advised on the west tower of Cobham Church: entirely feasible, since the Cobham family were also the lords of Cooling Castle and a power in the court. Yevele was awarded the Kentish manors of Tremworth and Vannes; he died in London in 1400.

to the choir, no more than 5ft wide and 12ft high, but enough to disclose the vista right through to the corona, more than twice the distance of the nave, beyond another flight of steps at the far end of the choir, beyond the 13th-century throne of Purbeck marble upon which archbishops are consecrated, beyond the spot in the centre of the Trinity Chapel where under a great 12-branched candelabra suspended from the vault an inscription in brass set into the stone-slab floor commemorates the shrine of Becket, beyond all this to the 13th-century east window, with its glass telling the narrative of the crucifixion, the entombment, the resurrection, the ascension, and pentecost, with Christ in glory.

At the end of the south aisle of the nave is the south transept, surviving work of Anselm but with a rose window pierced by William of Sens. Off the transept there is St Michael's Chapel, full of rich embellishment, banners of war, and, half in, half out in the close (the result of 15th-century rebuilding), the tomb of Archbishop Stephen Langton, the church's champion against King John: Langton signed the Magna Carta.

Move to the centre of the cathedral and look back at the great expanse of the west window: more famous glass, including the homely scene of Adam digging after the eviction from Eden ('When Adam delved and Eve span,/Who was then the gentleman?'). And immediately above the crossing is the soaring interior of Bell Harry with great springing arches and marvellously delicate tracery. Through the entrance in the stone screen, the choir is enclosed by an earlier stone screen. High up in the clerestory windows, more 13th-century glass, the narrative hardly discernible to the naked eye, but the colour still wonderful.

Out into the choir's south ambulatory, and you are first struck by the contrast: in the south-east transept (the ground plan of the cathedral is a double cross with two transepts on the south and two on the north) is glass executed in 1957 by Erwin Bossanyi with good intentions but sentimental draughtsmanship and bizarrely miscued colour; a shame in a cathedral where there is more fine medieval glass than anywhere but Chartres – in spite of the efforts of Oliver Cromwell's man, 'Blue Dick' Culmer, who boasted as he smashed windows of 'rattling down Becket's glassy bones'.

This part of the cathedral is the work of William of Sens. The whole east end of the cathedral was burnt down in 1174. William took on the task of rebuilding, basing it on his work in his home city. He was to have rebuilt the whole of the east end, the new Trinity Chapel to house the shrine of Thomas Becket, at that point still in the crypt. But when the choir was almost complete, he fell 50ft from the scaffolding and received injuries from which he never recovered. William the Englishman took over and unceremoniously altered the concept. He built a second flight of 16 steps so that he could make a new and taller crypt at the east end of the Norman crypt, and erect Trinity Chapel and Corona at this level. If William of Sens had intended something similar, it certainly was not to be done in this way, because as you climb the steps you can clearly see how the Englishman's work cuts across the last of the Frenchman's.

Just before William the Englishman's steps is the little chapel of St Anselm with a fine and remarkably complete wall painting of St Paul shaking off the viper. Up the steps and in the ambulatory are some striking monuments: and the first one is the most romantic. This is the tomb of the Black Prince, victor of Crecy and Poitiers. He lies clad in golden armour, his face flamboyantly moustachioed, replicas of his 'achievements' – helmet, breastplate, mighty double-edged sword, gauntlets – suspended

Lanfranc
Lanfranc, Archbishop of Canterbury born around 1005, became famous as a teacher in Avranches, and when he was 40 became prior at Bec, which was then still being built. In June 1066 William, still only Duke of Normandy, invited Lanfranc to become abbot of St Stephen's, Caen. In 1070, Lanfranc followed his liege lord to England as Archbishop. The role combined sacred duties with secular in a way inconceivable today. He was a superb politician and the chief counsellor to William, was often vice-regent in his absence from the country, and presided in secular courts; a position combining, in a sense, the roles of Prime Minister with Primate and Lord Chief Justice. He was powerful and popular enough to sue William's half brother, Odo, for the repossession of Kentish lands, and to win the case.

Tomb of the Black Prince

Archbishop Anselm
Archbishop Anselm was one of the three great Norman monks who became powerful in England after 1066. Unlike the other two, Lanfranc and Gundulf, Anselm was not a man of the world. Anselm was born in 1033, to a rich family in Aosta, north-west Italy. In 1060 he renounced wealth to become a monk at Bec in Normandy. When his superior, Lanfranc, left Bec for Caen, Anselm became first prior, then abbot. In 1093, Anselm reluctantly became Archbishop of Canterbury at an equally reluctant invitation from King William Rufus, who had been enjoying the wealth of Canterbury since Lanfranc's death four years earlier. He took the post on condition that William restored the church's land and liberties, and won the point after a long struggle. Anselm had none of Archbishop Lanfranc's political abilities, but he was certainly very brave: he continually rebuked William Rufus over his dissolute ways, risking regal displeasure to the point of being in mortal danger. After Rufus's death he continued to fight Henry I over the monarch's presumed right to appoint bishops: an old English custom that had no parallel in the rest of the Christian world. The king finally conceded the point.

Anselm was canonised in 1494; the papal relations had been seen to by Dante, who saw Anselm as being 'among the spirits of light and power in the sphere of the sun'.

above the tomb (the real ones, faded but impressive, are shown in a glass case nearby).

Next is the Corona with its view towards the west and its tomb with the remains of Reginald Pole, cardinal of the Roman church and Queen Mary's Archbishop.

Opposite Prince Edward is the sepulchre of the only monarch buried in Canterbury, Henry IV (usurper of the Black Prince's son, Richard II), with his queen, Joan of Navarre, both splendidly sculpted in alabaster. And by the north entrance to the choir is the tomb of Archbishop Chichele, who, like his successor Runcie, held a service of thanksgiving for a victory won (Chichele's for Agincourt, Runcie's for the Falklands). In a recess beneath Chichele's resplendently robed figure is a twin figure: his naked cadaver.

At the foot of the steps into the north transept is the spot where Thomas Becket was martyred; here too Archbishop and Pope renewed acquaintance in mutual prayer in 1982, the first occasion since Henry VIII took Ann Boleyn of Hever Castle to wife. Off this transept is the Angel Chapel, with delicate shafts leading to the first big fan-vault in England. And in this transept there is an entrance to the crypt.

The crypt is the finest in England, a great church in its own right. In this church lay Becket's body until its translation to the Trinity Chapel in 1220; and to this place Henry II came in sackcloth to do penance for his part in the murder of the archbishop. The crypt's massive solemnity is a wonderfully appropriate underpinning to the leaping Gothic above, and the fantastic variety of its ornamented and sculpted piers and capitals are a treasury of the Romanesque in themselves. In the apse of the Norman crypt is the chapel to Our Lady of the Undercroft, donated by Lady Mohun in 1396, and with an exquisite Perpendicular screen. Here too in recent years has been placed a bronze of the Madonna and Child which has a gentle sense of self-containment, gleaming in the semi-darkness of the niche above the altar. It was made by Sister Concordia, Prioress of the Abbey of Minster in Thanet.

East of this is the Trinity Chapel crypt built by William the Englishman in Caen stone like the rest of the cathedral but, as in the Trinity Chapel and Corona, he enriched the effect of its tall pointed arches with liberal accents in Purbeck marble, but practically no other decoration.

Ascending to the steps through the north doorway to the transept above, the door almost opposite leads to the cloister, again England's most glorious, of many periods but mostly early-15th century. Off the cloister, a comparatively small doorway opens into the chapter house, a vast, light room with a fine coffered wooden ceiling.

Eastwards from the cloister through the Dark Entry are the monastic ruins: the dormitories, the infirmary, the site of the cellarer's lodging, the infirmary hall and chapel. Most extraordinary of all is the water tower, not a ruin but Prior Wilbert's 12th-century construction for which the pre-1160 drawings still exist, more Heath Robinsonesque than Romanesque. Quaint, maybe, but the waterworks still work, daily and efficiently.

North of the ruins are the buildings of King's School, a jumble of medieval buildings, and modern restoration. As for the rest, Defoe wrote long ago:

'The close circumvallation, where the houses of the prebendaries and other persons belonging to the cathedral stand, is very spacious and fair, and a great many very good houses are built in it, and some with good gardens; where those gentlemen live at large, and among whom a very good neighbourhood is kept up.'

There is no improving on that description.

Becket's Shrine

'Good God!' Erasmus said when he saw the treasures at the shrine of Thomas Becket in Canterbury. 'What a display was there of silken vestments, what an array of golden candlesticks.' In 1538 Henry VIII declared Becket a traitor and sent in the royal receiver to collect the treasures. There were 310 pounds of gold, 276½ pounds of gilt plate, 52½ pounds of parcel gilt and more than 330 pounds of silver. The receiver left no record of the countless precious stones, though Erasmus had remarked that the least of the treasure was the gold: '. . . every part glistened, shone, and sparkled with rare and very large jewels, some of them exceeding the size of a goose's egg,' he said. The receiver needed 26 wagons to carry away all this treasure. Much of it turned out to be fake, but the donors had probably given it in good faith.

One genuinely precious item Henry reserved for his personal adornment. It was the so-called Regal of France, a great jewel given by Louis VII of France in 1179 after he had visited the shrine with Henry II, and passed the night in vigil. The Regal was mounted as a ring with a golden angel standing to one side pointing at the jewel. Henry wore it on his thumb.

THE STOUR VALLEY

Most visitors arrive and leave Canterbury along the A2, with the approach into the city along Rheims Way its own reward; the road itself is not beautiful (though a detour through Harbledown on the old Pilgrims' Way is), but there are breathtaking views of the cathedral. Still, the finest roads to Canterbury are the A28 from Ashford along the Stour Valley, and the A252 from Charing, which joins the A28 between Chilham and Chartham.

Towards the Ashford end of the Stour Valley **Boughton Aluph**'s handsome, isolated church stands surrounded by meadows; for a couple of weeks each June the supper marquees go up and that growing British pastime, the music festival, gets under way. This is one of the smallest and best, founded by the Deller family (there is a finely inscribed memorial plaque to Alfred Deller in the choir aisle of Canterbury Cathedral), totally professional and with a devoted following.

Chartham just about clings to its character as a village around a green, but its 13th-century church has a very handsome interior with a fine wooden raftered ceiling focused on a boss carved with oak leaves; there is a remarkable 6ft 3in brass of 1306, only a few years after the church was consecrated, to a crusader who fought with Edward I; and an eloquent marble memorial signed by JM Rysbrack in 1751 and erected by a gentleman of the parish in memory of the wife who died pathetically young.

A couple of miles along the Charing road is **Chilham**, one of the most perfect villages in England. So it has to protect itself with a pay-and-display car park just off the main road, though anyone who wants to start with Chilham Castle can park in the castle grounds. The village itself has timber-framed cottages surrounding a little square; the church off the north side of the square facing the castle to the south. I once brought a young Bulgarian here;

Chilham

she found it impossible to grasp that the
battlemented church was a church and not a
castle, and that the alleged castle was clearly
nothing more than a very grand house.

Two pretty streets lead east from the square
and that is it. Sir Dudley Digges, Master of the
Rolls, and Mary Kempe demolished most of
the original castle in 1616 – the keep remains
handsomely converted into living quarters –
and built instead an imposing dull brick
Jacobean house (not open) with huge
overbearing mullioned windows overlooking a
steep slope spaciously terraced in the same
brick, planted with roses, mulberry and
wisteria. Below this there are tall yew hedges
in a plantation of lime and beech, then comes a
rose garden, a herb garden, a vegetable garden
with a lake and the Stour gleaming far below.
There are wide lawns with stone urns planted
with pansies, handsome topiary, a haha, and
meadows beyond with sheep and cattle.

The garden can be visited, and also at the
castle is the 'Raptor Centre', a good place to
see birds of prey at close quarters. Injured
birds of prey are tended here, and there are
displays of falconry with talks on the subject.

Tradition has it that St Augustine's remains
were buried in Chilham church after the
dissolution of his abbey at Canterbury; there is
no proof but the church is indisputably
beautiful.

Downhill from Chilham the tiny village of
Godmersham has a church with strikingly
simple and beautiful lancets in the east end of
the chancel. At Godmersham Park, a Georgian
house guarded by 'alsatians trained to attack'.
Jane Austen used to visit her brother; here she
wrote *Pride and Prejudice*.

Three miles downriver from Canterbury the
A28 arrives at Sturry. Turn right and over a
little medieval bridge a ¼-mile away and in a
time warp (apart from the traffic queueing to
squeeze over the bridge) is the tiny village of

Fordwich, with grassy banks that were once wharves beside the churchyard, the pub, and the town hall. Here came the Caen stone for Canterbury Cathedral and St Augustine's, and the lead for their roofs. The town, as it was, was a 'limb' of the Cinque Ports, charged with supplying men for the navy and with fitting up half a ship. The church is full of character, with some 14th- and 15th-century glass in quatrefoil windows, 18th-century box pews, a big coat of arms and text painted in tribute to William of Orange, scourge of Papist James II, a square, primitive Norman font, and a Norman stone, once part of a tomb, carved with the fishscale pattern inseparable from Kent and East Sussex. The town hall has herringbone brick nogging infill between the timbers and on the first floor is the old courtroom with bar (hence 'the prisoner at the bar') and a small jury room. It may be England's smallest and oldest town hall.

Herne Bay

THANET

The Isle of Thanet is the old name for the north-east corner of Kent. It was cut off by the Wantsum Channel, once a formidable barrier and still only bridged in a handful of places. Today it is fringed by traditional seaside resorts.

Herne Bay

Like a respectable maiden aunt with the hint of a past, **Herne Bay** sits just the Canterbury side of Thanet, lifting her skirts clear of the pay-dirt of modern commercialism. When the British took their holidays in Britain, Herne Bay flourished. Those days are gone, but it is still proud; and its tree-lined streets are home not just to retired couples but to great bands of commuters to London as well. A lick of paint would see the front all right. As it is, there is a clock tower cumbersome as a portly mayor, built as the centrepiece when the resort was being planned in the 1830s. It has the kind of doric columns that gave Greek revival a bad name. But the front is wide and handsome and the town keeps its lawns and flowerbeds closely manicured.

Margate

Ten minutes down the fast A299 from Herne Bay, over what remains of the Wantsum Channel and into the Isle of Thanet proper, the action begins. Perhaps the long-stay customers don't come as much as before the sunshine package tours started, but the Kentish resorts are still full of life. And there is more affluence now than in the days when the boarding house landlady was queen of the holiday trade.

Margate, Broadstairs and Ramsgate sprawl around the coastline of north-east Kent with their slightly more stand-offish relations, like Westgate, Cliftonville and St Peter's. Of the three, **Margate** is the vivid sister, wearing a mask of paint over the genteel, even elegant features. Its Theatre Royal, recently restored, is the third oldest theatre in Britain. Margate claims the distinction of being the oldest seaside holiday town in England. Certainly it is the oldest on Thanet, flourishing long before even the invention of railways brought Londoners out by the thousand: in the early decades of the 18th century and continuing well within living memory, they came down the Thames by boat. In the 18th century Margate was a declining fishing village, though it had been a 'limb' of the Cinque Ports, expected to help to build and equip ships to keep out the French. In King Street, the Tudor House, a well-preserved beamed building of the 16th century, suggests how Margate might have looked. It houses the little local history museum. Beneath today's town it is easy to recognise the potential for fishermen in the little semi-circular bay with its lovely sandy strand rising to cliffs on the eastern side. But then a local man, Benjamin Beale, introduced the bathing machine to Thanet (like so many pre-Victorian entrepreneurs, he was a Quaker). The summer crowds arrived and the resort

Margate

Population: 54,980

Early Closing: Thu

Market Day: Mon (Apr–Sep)

Cashpoints: *Barclays* 64/66 High St; *Lloyds* 1 The Centre; *Midland* 12 The Centre, 244 Northdown Rd Cliftonville; *Nat West* 27 High St

Tourist Information: Marine Terrace

Attractions: Bleak House Museum, Dickens' House Museum, Margate Caves*, Shell Grotto*, Tudor House Museum

Arts: Winter Gardens, Theatre Royal

Leisure: Bemborn Brothers Theme Park, Hartsdown Park Sports and Leisure Centre

Cinema: Dreamland Cinema

By Road: London 76 miles (A28, A299, M2, A2), Canterbury 16 miles (A28)

By Rail: 1hr 30mins from London (London, Victoria to Ramsgate line). Direct services to Canterbury and Chatham. Connections to Dover via Ramsgate

Roads

When the M20 bypassing Maidstone was opened in 1960, it was the first major trunk road project, allowing for the Dartford Tunnel, since the arrival of the Romans. And even the M20 shadows the line on aerial photographs (taken by East Malling horticultural research station) which suggests that the Romans built a paved road between Wrotham and Maidstone. (An Anglo-Saxon document refers to the 'military road' between Leybourne and East Malling.) So adding this road to Watling Street (from Richborough through London to St Albans), and the ones from Canterbury to Lympne (the dead-straight Stone Street), from Canterbury to Dover, and from Rochester through Maidstone to Hastings, with branches to Reculver and from Canterbury through Wye to the old line of the Hastings road at Iden Green (where there is a paved Roman ford across a stream), you arrive at the rough basis of the modern road network. After the Romans left, their roads were grossly neglected and notoriously impassable in bad weather, to the point that Defoe recorded that a great oak for shipbuilding drawn on a cart by 22 oxen could take two or three years to reach Chatham 'for sometimes a whole summer is not dry enough to make the roads passable'. All this was changed by the various Turnpike Acts passed between 1709 and 1825 to set up toll roads.

grew. The houses of the period along the front are nicely proportioned and one or two still sport seaside regency rococo balconies. Just behind the front a house on the corner of Cecil Square carries the date 1769, when this square and Hawley Square were built (though Cecil Square also has a new shopping arcade with an electric five-bell carillon and a modern magistrates' court).

But the front is what people come for. It is alive with bingo, pool, amusement arcades, shooting galleries, fish and chip shops, lounging boys, and giggling gaggles of girls, sashaying along arm-in-arm; shops selling Margate rock, inflatable toys, brass and china ornaments, picture postcards.

The shop façades are lurid with promise. Appropriately, the biggest attraction is a fairground, or rather a 'theme park'. Bembons Theme Park covers some 20 tarmacadamed acres of what was once a bosky little park, and leaving aside the candyfloss and hamburgers ('McBemboms') they are dedicated to scaring seven kinds of living daylights out of their customers. And how youngsters (and adults) love it. In fact, this is one of Britain's biggest attractions, in the top-20 tourist ratings. There is a massive big wheel and a huge big dipper. Everything else is variations on a theme. You can do it in a water splash, you can do it upsidedown, you can do it in a chariot under the sightless gaze of gaudy 7ft Roman legionaries, you can do it in a Zeppelin or in a spacecraft.

In total contrast, four miles south-west of Margate, on the outskirts of **Birchington**, is the Powell-Cotton Museum, where the visitor is confronted by a remarkable display of stuffed animals placed in carefully re-created copies of their habitats. Major Powell-Cotton shot the animals in a series of big-game hunts during the later years of the 19th and early part of this century, but he acquired many other items on his travels and through auctions. Among them were 93 pieces of what have always been assumed were copies of Imperial Chinese porcelain. Authenticated in 1988, the collection is now recognised as the finest in Europe and includes 45 pieces made specifically for the Emperor and his family.

Broadstairs

Broadstairs is the classiest, as they say, of the Thanet holiday towns. There are touches of Margate in a few of the shops, but the town is more at home with the quieter bucket-and-spade brigade. And it has charm in buckets as well. It is a little like Brighton without the expansiveness or much of the Regency elegance: there are warrens of little alleys, 19th-century terraces, some older cottages and inns, some of the Dutch gables that in the east of Kent are a legacy of the Flemish refugees of the 16th century, a few handsome squares off the front, chalk cliffs enclosing a small boat-filled harbour, the famous North Foreland lighthouse of the 17th century (built soon after General Monck had rescued England's naval reputation by defeating Admiral de Ruyter in these waters) and, at the edge of the harbour, the brown and curious castellated house where Dickens lived while he wrote *David Copperfield*. Today it is open as a museum of Dickens and of maritime interest, and is known as Bleak House, though *Bleak House* was not written at the time Dickens lived there. The Dickens House Museum is sited in the house of Mary Strong, accepted as the original of Betsy Trotwood.

Dickens was everywhere in this town: he stayed at 31 High Street while he was working on *Pickwick Papers*, then he finished *Nicholas Nickleby* in what is now the Albion Hotel. Every summer there is a Dickens festival.

Ramsgate

Once a Cinque Port, once a trading port, famous for fish and infamous for smuggling,

The Saxon Shore

The Romans had little trouble controlling the enemy within during their rule of Britain from AD 43 until around 410. The enemy without was another matter. Hadrian's Wall, with its detachments of mobile Roman patrols, secured the North against tribal incursions, but increasingly the Saxons devastated communities in the south-east with hit-and-run raids in oar-propelled but streamlined warships, low and fast in the water. The British fleet, the Classis Britannica, operated out of Dover. Richborough was massively fortified in the third century and later Rochester too was pressed into service. But this proved insufficient and the Romans appointed a Count of the Saxon Shore to build a series of forts in a chain from the Wash (Brancaster) to Hampshire (Portchester), but concentrated in Kent. There were new fortifications at Reculver to guard the Thames estuary and the Wantsum passage, and at Lympne to hold the line between Dover and a new fort at Pevensey. The beginnings of this defence of the 'Saxon Shore' was not auspicious for the Roman Empire. The first Count, Carausius, proclaimed himself Emperor. Some of his coinage, and that of his successor Alectus, is in the British Museum. At the end of the third century, Roman law was re-established, and the Saxon Shore held until the Romans withdrew as their Empire came under increasing pressure.

Ramsgate

Population: 37,398

Early Closing: Thu

Market Day: Fri

Cashpoints: *Barclays* 11/13 Queen St; *Lloyds* 3 Queen St; *Midland* 1 High St; *Nat West* 53 High St, 52 Harbour Parade

Tourist Information: Argyle Centre, Queen St. Ferry Terminal, Port Ramsgate (summer only)

Attractions: Maritime Museum, Ramsgate Museum

Arts: Granville Theatre

Leisure: Conyngham Sports Hall, Dumpton Park Sports Centre, Ramsgate Swimming Pool

By Road: London 78 miles (A253, A299, M2, A2), Dover 20 miles (A256, A2), Canterbury 17 miles (A253, A28)

By Rail: 1hr 45mins from London (London, Victoria to Ramsgate line). Direct services to Canterbury, Dover and Margate

By Sea: Scheduled sailings to France

Ramsgate now is flush with holiday success. There is a picturesque harbour packed with yachts and other pleasure craft but with a large working harbour, Port Ramsgate, further down the quay. You can lean on the cliff railings high above and watch the sun-bound travellers: more people come to Ramsgate to sail away than stay.

And yet this is a good place, recognisably Kentish, solidly Victorian in the great brown stone arches built into the cliffs and used as workshops and retail stores by specialists in every marine requirement from sweaters and oilskins to sailmakers and engines for powerboats. There are two museums: one in the classical stone built Clock House, is the maritime museum opened in 1984. The Ramsgate Motor Museum on the Westcliffe Promenade has exhibits ranging from the Model T Ford to the ill-fated Sinclair C5. Up on West Cliff is the finest building in these parts. AW Pugin built himself a house here, solid and capacious with wide-ranging views of the sea. But beside it he built with £20,000 from his own fortune the church of St Augustine's. He began in 1845 and finished in 1850, and thereafter regarded it as his best work. With its squat tower, tall gables and steeply pitched roofs of grey fish-scale slates St Augustine's is an impressive homage to early Christianity in these islands; more akin in spirit to the little abbey of Iona than to any other building in Kent.

Driving south along the A256 towards Sandwich the visitor passes *Hugin*, the replica of a Viking Ship placed here in 1949 following a recreation of the landing by Danes 1500 years earlier.

On one side of Pegwell Bay is the site of the Hoverport which when active had remarkably little effect on the masses of migrating birds which each spring and autumn gather in the bay and on the Sandwich Flats at the mouth of the River Stour.

Reculver

When the Wantsum was more substantial, **Reculver** commanded the Thames estuary before the crossing into Thanet, so here the Romans built a great fort and settlement. A third of the area has been washed away, but one of the walls of the fortress is still there a little to the east of the church. The church itself, squarely inside the compound of the camp, is one of the early monuments of English christianity, founded by King Sigbert of Kent within a century of Augustine's death. The vicar and congregation decided by one vote in 1809 to knock it down and use the materials to build a smaller church more suited to their needs. Fortunately, Trinity House at Deptford built the great buttressing seawall to stop the rapid erosion of the shoreline and bought and preserved the West front of the church with the two great towers because of their usefulness as a landmark. Approached along the seawall from the car park, the towers are an extraordinary and eloquent monument to an age of newly renascent faith, as moving a sight, potentially, as Whitby Abbey or Iona. Below, however, is a caravan site with cafés, pool halls and bingo.

Almost due south of Reculver, across the A28, lies the quiet wetland area of Chislet Marshes. In the pub at Boyden Gate you can study photographs of many MCC teams – the initials stand for the Marshland Cricket Club.

At **Stodmarsh**, riverbank footpaths can be followed through a fascinating wetland area created from an area of mining subsidence. It is rich in marsh-loving plants and birds; among them, rarities such as Savi's warblers and bitterns find cover in the swamp, and masses of ducks and the odd predator may be seen. This National Nature Reserve is between the A257 and A28 roads.

Richborough

You can see Pugin's church of St Augustine on

Canterbury and Whitstable Railway

Like its predecessor, the Stockton and Darlington Railway of 1825, the Canterbury and Whitstable started life in most people's minds as a waterway. But after George Stephenson's pioneering success with the businessmen of Darlington, where *Locomotion No 1* hauled a heavy goods and passenger train at 15mph, railways were the coming thing. The Canterbury and Whitstable Railway, like the Liverpool and Manchester line, also employed Stephenson. Unfortunately, the *Invicta* that he built for Kent was nothing like as good as the *Rocket* (which attained a sensational 30mph), and because of the gradients on the line, trains had to be hauled by fixed engines for all but a mile of the 6-mile track. Still, on the tenuous grounds that the line opened a few months before the Liverpool and Manchester Railway, and that the Stockton and Darlington was primarily intended to haul coal to the Teeside docks, true sons of Kent proclaim theirs the first passenger railway in the world. The *Invicta* was retired in disgrace in 1839 and stands in Canterbury Heritage.

its clifftop from three miles distance at
Ebbsfleet, where Augustine is reputed to have
landed (and where the Danes did land), and a
little further south on a patch of high ground
there is the former Roman island fortress of
Rutupiae. The Wantsum now is swallowed by
the Stour long before **Richborough**. Close by is
one of Kent's larger caravan sites, by
marshalling yards, by the massive Richborough
power station (visible over a low hill from as
far away as Reculver), and by a spray of light
industry. But there is a picnic area where you
can sit with your back to all this and gaze out
to sea.

The fort's ruins are looked after by English
Heritage and are, apart from Hadrian's Wall,
the most impressive Roman remains in
England. The legions arrived here from Rome
and stayed for 400 years, and when the Saxons
began to attack, it became not just a staging
post for the legions and a great ordnance depot
but also a massive naval base under the
command of the so-called Count of the Saxon
Shore. The remains show evidence of the
original wooden stockade, of stone and tile
ramparts, of shops with verandas opening on
to Watling Street as it went through the west
gate, of latrines and of the commandant's
house. The stone walls still stand for long
stretches 25ft high. Some of the more precious
items found at Richborough have been shipped
to the British Museum, but what remains in the
little museum is fascinating, showing a
continuity in building materials, tiles, bricks
and nails, that reached forward to the mid-19th
century, when mass production began to
replace the blacksmith and the local brickyard.

Cooling tower, Richborough

Sandwich

When the Romans departed, the Saxons built a
small church within the fort of Rutupiae, but
their preference was for **Sandwich**. It was
Sandwice in Domesday from the Old English
for 'sand market town'. In 1086, when the

Domesday commissioners reported back to King William, Sandwich paid the same tax as Dover, plus 40,000 herrings for the monks of Christ Church, Canterbury. There were 383 dwellings. Today there are only twice as many, and still they do not fill the space within the town walls.

Is this the loveliest town in England? Certainly it is one of the most unspoilt. It does not live in the past, but it is a complete pre-industrial revolution settlement. St Clement's church is one of the biggest in the county, East Anglian in size and in the angels carved with wings outspread on the roof beams of the nave, and gloriously picked out from the gloom in gold. The massive Norman tower is fortress-like in proportions, and the only church tower to have survived in Sandwich: the tower of St Mary's collapsed and was not replaced; the tower of St Peter's collapsed and was replaced by a brick tower with a wooden cupola. St Peter's has never been deconsecrated but is now used by the tourist information office, and here in summer they distribute maps and a useful itinerary for an exploration of the town.

Sandwich repays almost as well aimless wandering, but any walk should certainly include the town walls, which are almost completely in park-like surroundings. There is also, at one point, a fine view into Gertrude Jekyll's garden for the Salutation, built in 1911 by Lutyens, its glowing orange brick melding harmoniously with the town.

To Sandwich came Cnut with his invasion force in 1013. Later in the Middle Ages, the town was twice sacked by the French and once during the Wars of the Roses. But it was the most important of the Cinque Ports and England's most powerful naval base. As the sea receded, the town's prosperity was restored by the Protestant refugees from France and the Netherlands. The marshes to the north

Flemings and Huguenots
Medieval immigrants transformed the economy of Kent. First, Edward III invited Flemish weavers over in the 14th century to modernise the backward English cloth manufacturing industry. Then in the 16th and 17th centuries, Flemings and French Huguenots fled to England and introduced new skills, even whole new industries. It was the Flemish who made hop cultivation a large-scale agricultural activity and who introduced commercial market gardening on the fields between Sandwich and Canterbury, flatlands still known by the Flemish name of 'polder'. The Huguenots set up the silk-weaving industry which prospered to such an extent (until the East India Company's activities dealt English silk a death blow in the 18th century) that in Canterbury alone it employed 2000 workers. Huguenots were so numerous in the city community that they were granted their own chapel in the cathedral which is still there, in the crypt. Flemish clothmaking also rescued Sandwich, whose harbour had silted up. And in Sandwich especially the Flemish left a mark on the county's architectural style, with curved brick gables that might have come straight out of a painting by Pieter de Hooch.

Whitstable Oysters
'The native Royal Whitstable oyster is dead. Long live the oyster'. Whitstable, once synonymous with the oyster, was by no means the only town in Kent associated with it. Defoe singled out Milton Regis and Faversham for special mention, but the Medway between Burham and Sheerness was a famous bed; there was another at King's Ferry in the Swale off Sheppey, another at Reculver, and the sea off Sandwich was a prolific source. Today, Whitstable is making a special effort to breed oysters again, propagating them scientifically and publicising them with an annual oyster festival. Part of the effort is aimed at making oysters a popular food once more, to rid them of their comparatively recent association with the champagne-swilling classes. The sites of Roman fortresses are often littered with oyster shells, and for centuries oysters were a working man's nourishment: in the 15th century Canterbury labourers are recorded as consuming 6 bushels of oysters for their dinners at a cost of 4s6d. Until World War I, Whitstable exported millions of oysters to the Continent and to the USA. Today, the best oysters in British restaurants are flown in fresh from Florida.

of Sandwich are still locally called polders, and of course there are many Dutch gables in the town, including one on a corner of St Peter's. Fishergate is the only remaining medieval gate into the city. The Barbican gate was built by Henry VIII. From 1127 Sandwich had the right to collect tolls on the ferry at this point, and at the Barbican tolls continued to be collected until 1977. A board fixed inside the gate by the Guildhall authorities in 1905 continues to detail the charges, ranging from 2s3d for every chariot, or other vehicle drawn by six or more horses or other beasts, to 2s for every horse or mule.

East of the town runs a famed trio of championship golf courses, Prince's, Royal St George's and Royal Cinque Ports, which bound the sea, running from Shell Ness Point to Deal. A walk along the foreshore beside Prince's towards the nature reserve at Shell Ness gives a fascinating insight into the plant and animal life of the dunes and salt marshes.

Whitstable

Whitstable, nearest of the coastal towns north and east of Canterbury, is also the one which nowadays makes fewest concessions to holidaymakers. Its eastern suburb of Tankerton has handsome grassy banks planted with shrubs sweeping down to the little beach, but no outward encouragement to anyone to do more than come and walk the dog or sit on a bench in the sunshine. The town itself is an incoherent jumble with suggestions of quaintness, and, at Sea Wall is the big old warehouse of the Royal Free Fisheries and Dredgers (incorporated 1793), the Whitstable Oyster Company, Pearsons Crab and Oyster House, and a scatter of pubs which all sell oysters. Every year in July sees the 'blessing of the waters' ceremony, a religious service on the foreshore, with a gathering of fishing boats.

2 Rochester, Chatham and North Kent

The M2 from Canterbury starts its descent into the Medway valley above Rochester 3 miles before the river crossing. The motorway is too busy for it to be a pleasant drive, but it is a thrilling descent, promising something sensational. And sure enough, where the Medway pushes north through the chalk escarpment towards the Thames the motorway bridge commands sweeping views up and down the river; the tallest Norman Castle keep on the east bank with one of the smallest cathedrals tucked in behind it on lower ground, the bridges between Rochester and Strood that have been there one way or another since Roman days, cement works, papermills, orchards, and oast houses marking the retreating tide of the hop gardens of Kent.

Rochester is the centre of a much larger urban complex, with Strood on the west bank of the Medway and Rochester High Street crossing by the railway and emerging on the other side at the ancient (founded 1124) but much altered chapel of St Bartholomew's Hospital to become Chatham High Street. Chatham merges seamlessly into Gillingham, itself indistinguishable from Rainham.

Rochester Castle

The great industrial focus of the area was the Royal Navy dockyard of Chatham: 500 acres of it. The Admiralty closed the yard in 1984 with the loss of 8,000 jobs. But instead of sinking to its knees, the local authorities have fought to attract fresh industry and to bring in the great invisible earner, tourism. At Chatham, the dockyard that built HMS Victory is open to the public for the first time in 400 years. And Rochester is playing its Dickens associations for all they are worth: as a national literary lion Dickens cuts across the barriers of class and education.

Rochester/Chatham

Population: 142,364

Early Closing: Wed

Market Day: Fri

Cashpoints: *Barclays* 263/265 High St Chatham; *Lloyds* 142/146 High St Chatham; *Midland* 87 High St Chatham; *Nat West* 188 High St Rochester, 148 High St Chatham

Tourist Information: Eastgate Cottage, Rochester

Attractions: *Chatham* Chatham Historic Dockyard*, Fort Amherst* (Gillingham), Royal Engineers Museum (Gillingham), Medway Heritage Centre. *Rochester* Charles Dickens Centre, Guildhall Museum, Rochester Castle

Arts: *Chatham* Central Hall Theatre, Medway Arts Centre, *Rochester* Medway Little Theatre

Leisure: Alpine Ski Centre (Gillingham), The Ice Bowl (Gillingham), Lordswood Leisure Centre (Nr Gillingham); Strood Sports Centre

Cinema: Cannon Cinema, Chatham

By Road: London 31 miles (A2), Maidstone 8 miles (A229)

By Rail: *Rochester:* 45mins from London (London, Victoria to Dover line). Direct services to Gravesend and Canterbury. *Chatham:* 1hr from London (London, Victoria to Dover line). Direct service to Canterbury. From both towns there are connections to Maidstone via Strood and to Sheerness-on-Sea via Sittingbourne

ROCHESTER

The easy approach to **Rochester** is not along the Roman Watling Street, the A2, because that is hopelessly snarled by the town centre traffic in Gillingham and Chatham, but from the motorway and through Strood to the bridge. A bridge was first built here by the Romans after Claudius defeated the Britons at this point: he had ordered his army to swim the Medway and take the massed British in the south flank. The first stone bridge was built in the 14th century. Today the oldest of the three bridges is the iron railway bridge of 1885. The other two, of 1914 and 1971, are for east- and west-bound motor traffic. Together, the three make an ignoble approach to a noble city.

After the cathedral, the starting point of any tour of the city must be the castle, its most imposing building. On this mound both the Romans and the Saxons built defensive works, though the Britons chose to defend the Strood bank of the Medway, fatally doubting the Roman ability to ford the river in good order. On any reckoning, Rochester was a key strategic and commercial centre. Right through until this century, the Medway was mid-Kent's best highway, and the parish records of villages round Maidstone are full of references to boatmen and sailmakers and their apprentices. From Rochester fruit and hops and fuller's earth went to London, Essex and the Continent; and to Rochester came imports from abroad and coal from Newcastle. Odo, the battle-axe wielding Bishop of Bayeux, as he was depicted on the Bayeux tapestry, coveted Rochester and assaulted the castle in 1088. Soon after, Gundulf built the fortress whose ruins now encircle a park. The present keep, 115ft high, turrets intact, the biggest and most complete Norman fortress in England, was added in 1127. The 113 steps from the first floor to the top are rewarded by wonderful views.

King John took the castle, with difficulty.

Roger de Leybourne held it for Henry III against Simon de Montfort in 1264. To great popular acclaim the rebel Wat Tyler took the castle in 1381. As Chatham shipyard grew and Rochester castle became outdated, other fortifications rose further downriver, though all failed ignominiously in 1667 when de Ruyter led a Dutch squadron into the Medway and laid waste to the pride of the English navy near *Upnor*.

The city grew up around cathedral and castle. Below them the High Street, now restricted for traffic, runs along an east-west axis. From the western (bridge) end, it has on the right hand of the street the Royal Victoria and Bull Inn. The least of it is that Victoria stayed here overnight as a young princess; Dickensians prize it more for its associations with *Great Expectations* and *Pickwick Papers*. It was built in the 18th century to cater for the stagecoach trade, and its central arch recalls those days. On the other side of the road, the florid Guildhall, 17th-century brick baroque, carries itself handsomely on a pillared arcade. The resoundingly named Sir Cloudesley Shovel, MP for Rochester and a sailor who did much service to the crown after the Restoration, paid for the beautifully plastered ceilings in the council chamber and committee room within. In 1706 he added the Corn Exchange further up the road with its extravagant doorway, dainty cupola, and spectacular clock overhanging the street. In this part of the street too, the George Inn has a medieval vaulted undercroft, not normally open to the public.

Beyond, the street called Northgate cuts across the High Street and turns into Boley Hill, which climbs up past the cathedral, passing by Chertseys Gate, one of the three remaining entrances to the dissolved St Andrew's Abbey (more Dickens associations here: Jasper's Gate in *Edwin Drood*). Lloyds Bank is like any other high street Lloyds; but

Dickens

'I have many happy recollections connected with Kent,' Charles Dickens once wrote, 'and am scarcely less interested in it than if I had been a Kentish man bred and born and had resided in the county all my life'. He came to Chatham as a boy because his father took a job as a clerk at the dockyard. The family lived at what is now 11 Ordnance Terrace. He honeymooned at Chalk, near Gravesend, often took his holidays at Broadstairs, and lived his last years at Gad's Hill. He died in 1870, and an artist who arrived having planned to draw him at work, drew his *Empty chair* instead. The Swiss chalet in which he wrote much of his work has been re-erected in Rochester's Dickens Centre. Many of Dickens's novels were set, if only partly, in Kent, from the early but great *Pickwick Papers* onwards. Part of the Dickens industry lies in identifying the settings for scenes in his novels: fruitless, in one sense, but fun because so many of Dickens's descriptions are so sharp. This is particularly true of famous places like Rochester Cathedral, or the Bull Inn in Rochester High Street and the Leather Bottle Inn and the churchyard at Cobham, or 'the narrow streets of Deal,' as they figure in *Bleak House*: 'and very gloomy they were, upon a raw misty morning'.

Gundulf, Bishop of Rochester

Gundulf had not been marked out as having a religious vocation, but when he was in his early 30s (he was born around 1024) he went on a pilgrimage to Jerusalem and the experience made him decide that he wanted to become a monk. In 1059 or 1060 he duly entered the monastery of Bec, and from there he went to St Stephen's in Caen. In 1076 the see of Rochester fell vacant, and Lanfranc, Archbishop of Canterbury, asked Gundulf to fill the post. The prospect was not inviting: the fabric of the church was in disrepair, it was not a monastical institution, and there were only five canons. But Gundulf was already known as a talented builder. He was instituted as bishop on 19 March 1077, and immediately began rebuilding. As well as rebuilding Rochester Cathedral, Gundulf designed the White Tower in London for King William I – this is still the core of the Tower of London. He built Rochester Castle at a cost of £60 at King William II's behest; and in West Malling, Gundulf built the lone tower now known as St Leonard's. It was then probably part of a roadside fortification and possibly Gundulf's home. He also founded Malling Abbey, consecrated in 1103. Attended by Archbishop Anselm, he died on 7 March 1108, aged about 84, and was buried in Rochester Cathedral.

in a previous house at this site James II skulked overnight in ignominy before taking ship to France in the face of the 'Glorious Revolution'. Further up is the Six Poor Travellers' House, founded by Richard Watts in the 16th century, and further still, Eastgate House (Westgate House in *Pickwick Papers* and the Nun's House in *Edwin Drood*). This is a big, spacious Tudor brick and timber house with fine ceilings inside, converted now for use as a Dickens centre, and in the garden is the Swiss chalet presented to Dickens and used by him as a summer studio in the grounds of his last home at nearby Gad's Hill. In the vicinity there are more, quite extensive, ruins of the medieval city walls.

Back up Boley Hill beyond the cathedral were (and are) the homes of the rich and the buildings of King's School. Near the castle, Queen Elizabeth I stayed in the house, now Georgianly encased, of Richard Watts (founder of the charity in the High Street) and proclaimed herself in Latin 'satis'. Ever since, this has been Satis House. Beside it is the Old Hall, a grand 16th-century house, and beyond the school a lovely, gently sloping, shady public park called the Vines, because here, in the days before the Plantaganets brought the vineyards of Bordeaux under English protection, the monks planted their vineyard. On the other side of the park is Restoration House, showily Elizabethan but named after the return to England in 1660 of Charles II, who is said to have spent his first night here. Confusingly, Dickens gave it to Miss Haversham in *Great Expectations* and called it Satis House. Off the precincts at the far side of the Vines is the 18th-century street called Minor Canons Row. Close by is Priors Gate, the most perfect gate remaining.

Rochester Cathedral

Rochester is the less famous younger brother of Canterbury. St Augustine founded it as England's second diocese in 604, only half a

dozen years after founding Christ Church
Cathedral at Canterbury. After the Conquest,
Archbishop Lanfranc appointed his friend
Gundulf, abbot of Bec and talented builder, to
be Bishop of Rochester. He quickly built a new
cathedral slightly to the east of the old one (the
Saxon apse is marked on the stone floor inside
the West door). When Canterbury became a
favoured place of pilgrimage, Rochester lagged
far behind in riches and suffered two
disastrous fires. Then in the early 13th century
a baker from Scotland, William of Perth, was
conveniently murdered in the city after an
overnight stay on his pilgrimage to the Holy
Land. His servant was convicted but a widely-
held and totally unsubstantiated theory is that
an over-zealous monk plotted the murder for
the greater glory of Rochester. Miracles began
to happen at William's tomb in the cathedral
and pilgrims came by the thousand to wear
down the steps. The offerings of the pilgrims
enabled the bishop to engage in the next great
rebuilding, which produced most of the finest
parts of the church, the presbytery, choir and
the transepts.

Rochester Cathedral

The most impressive aspect of the cathedral
is the West front. Here the four Norman
towers at the termination of nave and aisles
have been heavily restored, in part, indeed,
rebuilt. So, after a series of vicissitudes and
rebuildings in different styles, was the main
tower: small, squat, 19th-century, but a faithful
recreation of the original. The big West door
survives as it was originally built; and as it was
originally sculpted, for on this kind of
Romanesque surface sculpture is as integral to
the final effect as structure. The West front is a
solemn orchestration of blind arcading,
magnificently pierced by a great Perpendicular
window. The climax of the Norman work is the
encrustation of the doorway. King Solomon
and the Queen of Sheba flank the door,
standing in for colonnades, corbels at

their feet and at their heads. Christ in glory (headless thanks to Cromwell) surmounts the tympanum, supported by angels and the signs of the evangelists. Beneath them the 12 apostles on the lintel support the tympanum, and around them are five orders of arches richly carved with foliage, mythical beasts and semi-human beings: monsters, grotesques and reptiles. Together with the carved doorways of Patrixbourne and Barfreston, this is one of the finest Norman doors in Kent, and little else rivals them in all England.

Inside the west doorway the arcading is filled with mosaic recording the glorious service of Royal Engineers in the wars against Kaffirs, Zulus, Afghans and others, and the glass of the window is their memorial. But the most immediately striking thing is the Norman nave with a gallery running above it embellished with diaper patterning.

The nave vault and tower vault are oak, but the later eastern end is stone-vaulted and the crypt, with the vault springing from head-high capitals, is one of the finest in England.

Charles Dickens had wanted to be buried in the cemetery which is in the castle moat; he had to make do with Westminster Abbey and Rochester Cathedral had to make do with a memorial plaque in the wall of the south-west transept. The site of the tomb of William of Perth is lost. The most interesting of the remaining memorials, in the north-east transept, are to Bishop Walter de Merton, founder of Merton College, Oxford, who died in 1277, and to Bishop John of Sheppey (died 1370), whose walled up tomb was uncovered by the 19th-century restorer Cottingham with its paintwork in pristine condition, as it remains. Close by, opposite the bishop's throne at the east end of the quire, is part of a medieval painting of the wheel of fortune. The quire has some 13th-century wooden stalls, the earliest in England, and the wall paintings are a Victorian restoration of the original 14th-century painted motifs of alternate lions and fleur de lys (the arms of Edward III, father of the Black Prince). The splendid painted organ on top of the quire screen was placed there by Sir George Gilbert Scott, who was responsible for the most obtrusive of the 19th-century restoration and for the Victorian kitsch high altar and reredos in the presbytery. But to end on a high note: the decorated doorway to the chapter room off the south-east transept is a glorious flowering of 14th-century sculpture, with foliage gathering to a pointed arch and the two largest figures flanking the doorway representing the synagogue blindfold and the church triumphant (Mosaic and Christian law).

Whatever can be said about Rochester Cathedral in the round, the scatter of sculpture throughout the building is its most engaging aspect. Some of the heads are carved with astonishing sensitivity and must have been portraits of townspeople or servants of the cathedral and monastery; one at the corner of the north-west transept and the north quire aisle, is a caricature of a grinning workman that looks as though it has been knocked off with the chisel in a matter of minutes. Faces and place are friendly: beyond the presbytery is the St Andrews's Centre, built as the deanery in the 17th century and now run as an education centre, where you can buy a cup of tea and homemade food (children welcome). If you bring your own picnic, you can eat it in the Centre's garden or the cloister garth, a quiet garden hemmed in by the Roman city wall on the south and the lovely ruined arcading of the chapter house built by Gundulf's successor Ernulf. The homely bronze of Mary and the Child Christ was placed there in 1980 to mark the 850th anniversary of the consecration of the cathedral. Though this is the heart of a diocese, it feels – in its sense of intimacy – like a big

Odo and Bayeux
The Bayeux Tapestry is neither French nor a tapestry. It was commissioned by Bishop Odo of Bayeux, Earl of Kent after 1066, to commemorate the Conquest, and it is a vast frieze (224ft 3 3/8in long by up to 21in in depth) embroidered on linen by Canterbury needlewomen, probably nuns. It tells the whole story of the events leading to the Battle of Hastings and of the battle itself more fully than any other source: much more fully than the laconic three-sentence entry in the *Anglo-Saxon Chronicle*. Stylistically it is a unity, and the design is dynamic, sophisticated, and highly competent, so that it is generally accepted that one Anglo-Saxon artist was in charge of the project. The artist was familiar with the Romanesque style, which was already widely disseminated in south-east England, especially Kent, before the Conquest.

Odo was the younger half-brother of William. In the tapestry he is shown clad in full armour and wielding a mace as he rallies fleeing Norman troops. He was born in the 1030s. After the Battle of Hastings, William awarded him a third of the land in the county, including Dover Castle. He was second in power to William. But Odo's ruthless depredations caused William to arrest him personally and have him imprisoned in Rouen for four years. On his release, he plotted against William Rufus, and had to flee to France. He died in 1097.

Prior Ernulf
When Prior Ernulf's choir at Canterbury Cathedral was first dedicated in 1130, after his death, William of Malmesbury wrote: 'Nothing like it could be seen in England either for the light of its glass windows, the gleaming of its marble pavements, or the many coloured painting which led the wondering eyes to the panelled ceiling above'. The crypt beneath survived a 13th-century fire as Ernulf's greatest monument. Only the crypt of St Peter's, Rome, is bigger than Canterbury's; but none is finer, not Chartres, not Rouen, not St Peter's itself. Ernulf (1040–1124) was a younger contemporary at the abbey of Bec in Normandy of Lanfranc and Anselm. In 1170 he joined Archbishop Lanfranc at Christ Church, Canterbury, and in 1089, under Anselm, he became prior. Ernulf was not himself an architect, but through his determined patronage he became known as a great builder. From Canterbury, Ernulf went as abbot to Peterborough and then in 1114 he returned to Kent as Bishop of Rochester: here, too, three arcades of the crypt are witness to his work. He was an authority on canon law, and in the library of Rochester Cathedral is the great compilation started by Ernulf of papers on law, on the church in Rochester, and on English and ecclesiastical history, the *Textus Roffensis*. It contains some of the finest English illuminated script.

parish church, a school chapel, even, since Rochester's King's School has daily services there, as well as big events like prizegivings. Rochester's cathedral is smaller than Canterbury's – 305ft against 517ft – the latter being particularly long. And when it was first built the nave of the cathedral did indeed double up as the parish church, but this was commonly the case with monastic buildings. The 15th-century church dedicated to St Nicholas that stands cheek-by-jowl with the cathedral was built to give the parishioners their own place of worship after endless squabbles with the monastery over the use of the cathedral.

CHATHAM

Rochester decks itself out with wine-bars and delicatessens, a brick-paved, traffic-free High Street, geraniums and petunias in baskets; **Chatham** works for a living and shows the marks on its face: wear and care. A thin measure of charm and quaintness coexist with tat, old pubs and weatherboarded houses with jerry-built shop fronts. Demolished buildings are roughly levelled into car parks and the High Street is choked with traffic, though towards the eastern end BBC Radio Kent has been handsomely rehoused in new brick-and-timber-clad buildings on the old Sun Pier, with a fine vista past the sailing barges moored in Limehouse Reach towards Rochester castle and cathedral. From here the road escapes the throng and follows the hairpin course of the Medway to the ornate main gate of the impressive Chatham dockyards.

The dockyards were built in 1719 and George III's coat of arms in Coade stone was added in 1811, but the yard was actually founded by Henry VIII in the year of his death, 1547, for the repair of ships and succour of the navy. In 1570 when William Lambarde wrote his account of Kent (confusing Chatham and

Gillingham as readily as any visitor today), he was so impressed by the sight of shipping in Chatham reach that he was able to write, with pardonable hyperbole:

No Towne, nor Citie, is there (I dare say) in this whole Shire, comparable in right value with this one Fleete: Nor shipping any where els in the whole world to be founde, either more artificially moalded under the water, or more gorgeously decked above . . .

Through the age of sail and the age of steam Chatham remained at the heart of Britain's domination of the sea. In 1586 Chatham built the *Sunne*, the first of 400 warships to be launched here. In the 17th century Chatham was the principal fleet anchorage. In 1759 Chatham's shipwrights built the Royal Navy's single most famous ship, *HMS Victory*. In 1863 Chatham became the first royal dockyard to build an ironclad. In 1908 Chatham began building submarines. The *Okanagan*, built for the Royal Canadian Navy and launched in 1966, was the last to be built here.

Visitors today do not enter the dockyard by the main gateway, but through a side entrance a ½-mile further on. The vast open spaces of the yard have the sadness of all great abandoned enterprises. You don't have to be a chauvinist to feel that in these crumbling dry docks, behind the grim institutional dignity of the great factories, the ropery, the lead and paint mill and the covered slips, lies crumbling also some of the maritime greatness of the nation. To some extent, the impression is false: when the Royal Navy abandoned the dockyard in 1984, most of its work had been concentrated in the Victorian extension to the dockyard. What is now open constitutes not only the most complete 18th and early 19th-century group of dockyard buildings, but also a greater concentration of listed buildings in this near 70 acres than anywhere else in Britain.

Standing in a spacious garden, the finest is the Commissioner's House, built in 1703 and embellished with a ceiling painting by Hogarth's father-in-law James Thornhill (who also painted the great ceiling in the Maritime Museum at Greenwich). The most impressive is the ropery of 1786–92, 1140ft long (not far short of a ¼-mile), and still working: some of the machinery was so well-manufactured that it has lasted since the beginning of the 19th century. Inside the main gate is the elegantly colonnaded guardhouse, built in 1764 for the Marines, and just opposite a big, plain, yellow brick church with galleries built by French prisoners of war in 1810, now rarely used for services, but often for rehearsals and performances by a local choral society and orchestra. There is a grand terrace of houses for officers, number 2 dry dock, where *Victory* was built, and adjoining it a dock where the hulk of the *Gannet*, an iron ship built in 1876 to be powered by sail and steam, is being restored over the next few years. For the history of architecture the most significant group of buildings is the group of covered slips (where ships could be built indoors), ranging from the first built during the Napoleonic Wars and looking like a vast wooden marquee, to the last of 1855, maybe the very first framed building as modern engineers and architects understand the term.

On the hill above the docks is Fort Amherst, an 18th-century warren of underground powder magazines, storerooms, bomb shelters, messrooms, barracks, and, above ground, bastions and gun batteries. It was, like the church in the dockyard, built by French prisoners of war as a defence against *le petit caporal*, Napoleon.

The A226 west from Chatham and Rochester shortly runs up **Gad's Hill**, notorious in history and literature for highwaymen and

Cobham Church

for Falstaff's ignominious encounter with them; and because Charles Dickens lived out his last years here at the top of the hill. Beyond Higham a country road runs through Shorne and over the A2 to **Cobham**. This is still Dickens country: the picturesquely half-timbered Leather Bottle looks quintessentially Pickwickian and in fact does play a part in *Pickwick Papers*. The whole of this pretty village, mostly stretched along the High Street, has been declared a conservation area, though too late to prevent some ostentatious modern houses making inroads on its visual integrity.

The church sits above the High Street, big and impressive; even more so inside with ornate piscinia and canopied sedilia in the chancel and the curious remains of a stone newel staircase which, it is thought, once led to a loft above a now-vanished screen. But Cobham church is famous mostly for its 17 brasses, most of them grouped together, all in good condition, many of very fine artistic quality. They mostly commemorate members of the Cobham family; the oldest, that of Joan de Cobham, is dated early in the 14th century. There is also a large handsome memorial of 1561 to the 9th Lord Cobham placed in the middle of the chancel before the altar, and with little figures of his many children kneeling around the base.

To the south of the churchyard is Cobham College, a little group of 14th-century buildings adapted in the 16th century as almshouses from their original purpose as a college for five priests to say prayers for Lord Cobham's soul. They remain almshouses to this day. The remaining courtyard (one is ruined) is open to the public and is an astonishing and historic survival in a small village: in feel and plan like a scaled-down courtyard of Merton College, Oxford.

The Cobham family seat was south of the village in Cobham Hall, Kent's biggest

The Paper Industry
All that is needed to make paper is a wooden frame with a fine-mesh screen stretched across it so that particles of mashed up rag or wood pulp catch in it and gradually build up into a sheet, and a constant flow of pure, clean water. So, though it might have been the accident of proximity to London that made Dartford the first place where paper was manufactured successfully in England (by John Spielman, granted a monopoly by Queen Elizabeth in 1589, and knighted for his success by James I in 1605) Kent, with its hundreds of watermills on little streams, became a natural home for the industry. Until then England had depended on French manufacturers for fine white paper. The expulsion of the Huguenots meant a big influx of papermakers into Kent, the secure foundation of an industry, and the creation of a new and unsung kind of male and female labourer who lasted well into the 20th century, shredding filthy rags to be rendered into pulp and choking their lungs on the particles. The most famous of the new papermakers was James Whatman, who took over an old cloth-fulling mill at Boxley in 1740 and made fine papers which are manufactured to this day, though now on a different site. The second impetus came with the popular press. Today, the great Bowater and Reed International mills at Sittingbourne and Aylesford (respectively) are the successors.

Popular Uprisings
Three great popular uprisings centred on Kent. Wat Tyler led the first. A pub of that name in the middle of Dartford supports the common belief that he was a Dartford man, but there seem to have been two or three Walter Tylers involved in disturbances at the time, so the stories told may involve a composite figure. One of the chief grievances in the peasants' revolution of 1381 was the poll tax. The rising began in Dartford but spread in September through all Kent. Tyler led up to 100,000 men over Blackheath to Smithfield, where as he was confering with King Richard II he was slain by the Lord Mayor of London.

Jack Cade led Kentish men in the rising of 1450 (over alleged oppression by Henry VI and local landowners). Cade gathered a force of 20,000 on Blackheath. The gates of London were opened for them by supporters, and for three days they occupied and looted the city. The rebels were offered pardons in return for going home, whereupon Cade led his men back to Kent and attacked Rochester Castle. Four days later he was hunted down and killed.

The third rising, in 1830, featured mass rick burning often accompanied by letters signed 'Captain Swing'. It was fomented by post Napoleonic-war depression, and revolution was widely feared.

Elizabethan house and grand by any standards. It was built between 1584 and the end of the century. Later, the names of Inigo Jones and John Webb were associated with it, but if they drew plans, nothing was executed. Today it is a girls' school, and the daily clutter of education doesn't sit well with how the other half lived; but many of the suites containing decor by James Wyatt have been kept in as near original condition as they can be. The park, once 1800 acres, now severely reduced, was landscaped by Humphry Repton and though bedraggled remains very beautiful.

London's commercial and industrial prosperity has reached out along the Thames from Woolwich through Erith and Dartford as far as Gravesend. **Dartford** people talk of 'going up the road' when they want to visit London: Blackheath is 20 minutes away. Dartford is the lowest point at which the Thames is crossed (by increasingly congested toll tunnels). Its long history has been all but obliterated under later building. But historic it is, having grown up around Watling Street's crossing of the River Darent. There is a pretty, car-free High Street, and in Holy Trinity Church Sir John Spielman is buried. He brought the paper industry to Kent where it flourished in countless villages whose watermills had previously been used for grinding corn. In Dartford it grew into a major industry, which it remains, and the drug industry has a base here as well.

Edward III founded a Dominican nunnery in Dartford, which after the dissolution became a royal residence on the road to Dover where Henry VIII and Elizabeth I sometimes stayed and where Anne of Cleves died. There are a few remains of the priory perimeter wall in Kingsfield Terrace. Dartford's most famous son made his mark in the reign after Edward III: Wat Tyler led the revolt in 1381 against the iniquitous poll tax. The pub named after him in the middle of the town is part of two or three nice streets of cottages built in the traditional Kentish style: brick, tile and weatherboard. The enterprising local authority has in recent years built a theatre here, the Orchard, as a North Kent base for drama, music and dance. North of Dartford the suburbs peter out in little alleys stretching fingers into the Thames-side marshland, criss-crossed by pylons stalking towards the river.

Gravesend, too, has seen better days. It was always a key point for Thames river traffic where Channel pilots change places with the so-called 'mud pilots' who guide ships going up-river. Here kings and potentates used to embark for foreign parts. And here in the church of St George, the Red Indian Princess Pocahontas is buried. She had saved the life of John Smith, founder of Virginia, but later, in the belief that Smith was dead, married John Rolfe and came with him to London. Legend has it that she discovered in London that Smith was still alive and after deciding to leave England, died of a broken heart at Gravesend. Grittier reality insists that she was already mortally ill when she arrived at Gravesend to embark for America. There is a bronze statue to Pocahontas in the churchyard.

Gravesend has a big Asian population and remains a place of faintly exotic character, with a High Street whose northwards vista is often filled by vast ships sailing to and from Tilbury on the Essex bank opposite. The waterside is crowded with wharves, mostly busy, and there is a pier, the old customs house, a pub, the Three Daws (featured in stories by Joseph Conrad), and a park converted from the fort where Gordon of Khartoum lived when he was in charge of the Thames defences. Even earlier, and surviving more completely, is Milton Chantry, founded by Aymer de Valence as the chapel of a leper hospital. It is now run by English Heritage as an arts centre; its best

feature is the original medieval timber roof construction of 1322. Out through the back streets east of Gravesend is a little pub called the Ship and Lobster, half on, half off the sea wall, with one bar consequently opening from the other up a steep flight of steps. On a sunny day this is a wonderful place from which to watch the sea-bound shipping on the Thames.

Between Dartford and Gravesend the church of St Mary the Virgin at **Stone** is on the road to nowhere. It is a detour to a dead end, surrounded by old cement works and houses of various post-war vintages, with tantalising glimpses of the industrial Thames at Long Reach far below. But it is a detour well worth taking. From outside the church is a hump-backed oddity, with chancel roof high above the nave. Inside it is a church of extraordinary finesse and artistry. The parishioners call it 'little Westminster Abbey'. It was built, mostly, in 1260, when Westminster Abbey was being rebuilt for Henry III, and must surely have been commissioned by the Bishop of Rochester, Lawrence de St Martin, who had a residence in Stone, was the king's chaplain, and shared the king's artistic tastes. So the church was built by the Westminster masons with a stone-vaulted chancel. John Newman, the great authority on Kent buildings, concludes from internal evidence that some of the beautiful arcade tracery in the chancel was actually carved at Westminster to measurements supplied from Stone, and shipped out to be fitted to the chancel walls.

The articulation of the piers in the nave with Purbeck marble shafts is echoed by the shafts of the blind arcading in the chancel and by the windows at the east end of the nave aisles, with separate internal stone framing and shafts. There is an abundance of carved stiffleaf vegetation, a number of heads in the corbels of arcades and windows sculpted with undemonstrative, highly skilled and sensitive naturalism.

Church font, Stone

FAVERSHAM

Faversham is still a small port, its wharves stacked with imported timber. But its corporate seal, made in the 13th century, boasts of much more: *'Regis ut arma rego libera portus ego'* – 'Since at my own expense I provide his armament I am the king's port'.

It lies on a creek of the Swale, the passage of water that separates Sheppey from the rest of Kent just as the Wantsum used to give Thanet a separate identity. Its boast in the time of Edward I was the culmination of long years of royal favour. King Stephen founded the Abbey of the Holy Saviour and was buried there; at the dissolution the bones were dug up and thrown in the river, but a loyal local retrieved them and reburied them in an unknown tomb in the parish church. When Henry VIII dissolved the abbey (it has since been all but obliterated), his charter to the town gave it wide powers, including the power of life and death in its court.

Like most Kentish towns, Faversham works for its living. Despite the pastel-painted houses in the lovely town centre, there is no sense of a community living off its past, though the past still lives. When Defoe journeyed through Kent, it was Milton, nearby, and Faversham that he mentioned for their oysters, not Whitstable. There are oysters still, and narrow streets leading down to the creek like Smack Alley and Quay Lane assert Faversham's water-based identity. When James II fled from London before William's advancing army and was captured he was identified by one Richard Marsh who took him to his house in Abbey Street where, though a prisoner, the king was treated with dignity. (James was returned to London, but fled again, to France.) Richard Marsh was later to found Shepherd Neame's brewery in the town. Brewing, and Shepherd Neame, is still a staple. Even today the house is part of the brewery and the main office

Lost Kent

The great erosion of Kent has not been by the sea along the northern coast, but by the spread of London. Lambarde wrote in 1570 that Kent 'extendeth in length from the west of the landes in Beckenham . . . where is the stile, as it were, over into Surrey, to the Ramsgate in the Isle of Thanet, about fiftie and three myles'. Even in this century, Kent included Bromley, the Crays, Orpington, Chislehurst and Sidcup. But the earliest towns swallowed by London were the nearest. There was Eltham, with its royal palace; Deptford, whose riverside alleys describe the exact lines of the old country lanes, where Christopher Marlowe is buried, where the prentice hand of Grinling Gibbons practised in the parish church of St Nicholas, and where the diarist John Evelyn lived on a grand estate by the river (borrowed once by Peter the Great of Russia); and there is Greenwich. Henry VIII was born in the palace at Greenwich and so was his daughter, Elizabeth. The new palace, begun by James I and completed by William and Mary, is one of the most stirring sights in the world – either from the hill above bisected by the meridian, or from the Isle of Dogs across the river.

building is next door, its four street-front pilasters gorgeously embellished in 1869 with plaster hop bines in full fruit.

A distinctly more dangerous commercial venture was the manufacture of gunpowder with which Faversham was for long associated. To appreciate the dangers involved we can turn to Defoe again:

While I was near this town some years ago, a most surprising accident happened, namely, the blowing up of a powder-mill . . . ; the blast was not only frightful, but it shattered the whole town . . . ; also several people were killed at the powder-house itself . . .

Pump, Faversham

Other serious explosions occurred at Faversham in 1767, 1781 and 1847. Demonstrations of gunpowder making (using inert compounds) are given at the restored Chart Gunpowder Mills on the edge of town. Gunpowder manufacture, as elsewhere in Kent, has ended; but there was and still is a shipyard. On royal favour, geographical position and commerce was built a town that is still one of the most delightful in the country.

The Market Place is dominated by the Guildhall, handsomely supported on an open arcade built in 1574: the hall itself is a replacement of 1819, nicely proportioned, confidently unassertive. In front of it is a gaudy 19th-century water pump. Around the Guildhall are several buildings built in Tudor times and even earlier, and east and west of the market place are streets with many fine 18th-century houses. But the prize runs north from the Market Place, at first as Court Street, and then as Abbey Street. Except where a couple of gaps have been filled, Abbey Street is a long vista of 17th- and 18th-century houses with some of the 16th century: one of these, number 80, is famous as the house built by 'Arden of Faversham' in 1538–40. Richard Arden was mayor of Faversham and was murdered in this house in 1551 by his wife and her lover, an event that is recounted in Holinshed's *Chronicles* and which inspired the Elizabethan verse drama.

The other big brewery, once the local firm Fremlin, now Whitbread (though they have kept the name of the brew), is opposite Shepherd Neame. Down the street beside it opens a sight of the unexpectedly tall church. In the north transept on one pier is a wonderfully preserved series of paintings of scenes from Christ's life of around 1310, and the misericords of the choir stalls are a riot of medieval incident: gryphons, dragons, birds, apes, women with winged heads and a devil dragging the innards from a man.

On a fork of Faversham Creek lies **Oare** with an approach to one of its pubs, the Shipwrights Arms, which is arguably the bumpiest of any in the land. There is a tiny Kent Trust for Nature Conservation reserve at Oare, but the better known reserves are **South Swale** to the north-west of Faversham and **The Swale** beyond Oare. In some winters, South Swale may attract as many as 500 Brent geese while the wider range of habitat at The Swale ensures an impressive variety of bird and plant species. Both are accessible along public rights of way but permits are required for visitors wishing to enter the reserves. The remarkable Saxon Shore Way – 140 miles of coastal path from Gravesend to Rye – winds along the edge of the Swale channel and in and out of Faversham. The path takes its name from the Roman fortifications against Saxon invasion. A walk towards Graveney Marshes can be both dramatic and surprisingly lonely under winter skies.

Back on the A2, on the outskirts of Faversham, is **Ospringe** with its famous Maison Dieu. Here any wayfarer, not just pilgrims, could find lodgings and hospitality. Only a timber-framed hall (of a later date) now

Country Parks
In Kent there are 40 country parks, from Ide Hill in the west to St Margaret's Bay in the east, and the Leas and Clifftop, Minster-in-Sheppey in the north to Park Wood, Kenardington (near Tenterden) in the south. The most westerly, Toys Hill, suffered badly in the October 1987 storm, which flattened practically every tree there. The country parks vary in location from Trosley Country Park, spectacularly high on the North Downs above Trottiscliffe and the Coldrum Stones, embracing areas of the North Downs Way and the Pilgrims' Way, to the picnic site overlooking Pegwell Bay, once painted by Frith, later a base for cross-Channel hovercraft. They range in size from the two-acre Pillory Corner picnic site overlooking Bewl Bridge Reservoir to the 2300 acres of Bedgebury Forest, clasping within it the 100-acre Bedgebury Pinetum. Kent County Council issues a list of the sites including a map.

stands on the site of the monastic hospital founded by Henry III – it is used as a museum.

A few miles west along the A2 are **Sittingbourne** and **Milton**, their old identities merged and submerged in commercial and industrial sprawl, though each still has a good church. Much of this sprawl can be seen from the Sittingbourne & Kemsley Light Railway as it carries passengers the 2 miles from Sittingbourne to the giant papermill at Kemsley. On the opposite bank of Milton Creek on the edge of Sittingbourne is Dolphin Yard, sole survivor of the 11 boat-building yards which once produced the red-sailed Thames barges. Since 1970 it has housed a museum dedicated to these much-loved vessels, several of which are tied up alongside the yard.

As a total contrast, it is possible on summer Sundays (not August) to stroll in the beautiful woodland garden of **Doddington Place**, a few miles south and over the bustling M2. West along the A2 from Sittingbourne is **Newington**, a place where miracles were often recorded by pilgrims in the years following St Thomas's murder. A little south is **Hartlip**, with an anchorite's cell set in the north tower of the church; the cell is now used as the vestry. North is **Lower Halstow** where pieces of Roman pottery still turn up on the marshes. Many tiles have been absorbed into the walls of the church over the centuries but it is the font which draws visitors to this surprisingly remote spot. Heavy guns were sited here in World War I and the vibration caused the plaster around the font to crack. Under it was a charming 13th-century lead font with kings and angels in its bays. It may lack the sheer exuberance of the font at *Brookland* but it wants for nothing in romance. West is **Gillingham**, seemingly always in the shadow of Rochester and Chatham next door; since the coming of the motorway even the traffic which once clogged its hills in summer bypasses it. Here, on the edge of the River Medway, the local council have created Eastcourt Meadows Country Park. The name is a little grand, but the views over Bartlett Creek and various marshes and islands are good.

THE HOO PENINSULA

North through Strood, the Hoo peninsula deserves better than it has got: ugly stock-brick villages, half-hearted strips of ribbon development and massive oil refineries. There are token references to the hinterland of Kent: hop kilns, oast houses, orchards and a few low, pretty hills. But this Thames marshland stands apart. It can, in fine days in spring and summer, seem benign, with marsh birds calling and the sun shining on the green crops. But it must live with the reputation given to it by Pip in *Great Expectations*:

. . . the dark flat wilderness beyond the churchyard, intersected with dykes and mounds and gates, with scattered cattle feeding on it, was the marshes . . . the low leaden line beyond, was the river . . . the distant savage lair from which the wind was rushing, was the sea.

As always, Dickens was writing fiction, so the endless game of trying to pinpoint the places he wrote about is no more than that. Still, he often used to walk to **Cooling** from his house at Gad's Hill, and the churchyard there contains 13 little chest tombs side by side, all children, all under 2 years old, all from one family, all dead of the marsh fever, Kent's malaria. Too improbable for fiction, so Dickens reduced the tombs to five and made the victims Pip's brothers. The churchyard is only 20ft above sea level, and northwards to the Thames stretch Cooling marshes.

What played no part in Dickens's tale is Cooling's greatest surprise, the castle. Its gateway, entire and undamaged, stands by the roadside, massive and machiolated. This is all that photographs normally show, but extensive curtain walling still remains surrounding a beautiful (and private) lawn: within the castle confines is a private house, ultra-suburban, but somehow the total contrast has great charm. Lord Cobham built the castle in 1381 as a defence against French marauders and fixed on the gateway a copper plaque that can still, with difficulty, be read:

Knouwyth that beth and schul be
That I am mad in the help of the cuntre
In knowyng of whyche thyng
Thys is chartre and wytnessyng

Later the castle was owned through marriage to Lady Cobham by Sir John Oldcastle (immortalised by Shakespeare as Falstaff). However, his fiery relationship with the Prince of Wales, later Henry V, and associations with the ideas of the heretic Wycliffe had deep repercussions, not least for himself: his life ended on the gallows at Tower Hill. In the 16th century another Lord Cobham was Sir Thomas Wyatt's uncle and he surrendered the castle to his nephew after a brief siege during the latter's uprising against Queen Mary.

West of Cooling, unlovely **Cliffe** has a big, fine 13th- and 14th-century church. Beyond the church lie a series of pools, created by the extraction of clay for cement making. It is possible to walk out to the sea wall and continue along paths around these pools studying the various birdlife and the proximity of East Tilbury Marshes across the busy Thames. To the east, the road runs to High Halstow, and a path leads to **Northward Hill**, an RSPB bird reserve, where Britain's largest heronry can be observed from a distance.

North-east, the road winds to the Isle of Grain, once but no longer separated from the rest of the peninsula by the Yantlet creek, and to the village of **Grain** itself. This small

Northward Hill – heron

community is overshadowed by the vast unco-ordinated spread of the BP refinery and the Central Electricity Generating Board's massive high-tech power station close by, sombre and splendid, designed by Farmer and Dark, overlooking the mouth of the Medway. The walk to the little strand opposite is popular with Sunday walkers; across the water at Sheerness, Kent's second most busy port after Dover, they can see the big Olau Line ferries getting up steam for the voyage to Flushing.

The peninsula holds one other surprise. At the end of a lane leading to the Medway not 10 minutes drive from Strood is **Upnor**. The little High Street runs sharply downhill to the Medway flanked by brick and weatherboarded cottages, shops and pubs. At the bottom is a brick and glass gazebo and a cottage gate with a 10ft wooden rudder as a hinge. It looks like a Kentish version of a North Yorkshire or Cornish fishing village, but this street grew solely to service the fort built by Elizabeth I to protect her naval dockyard on the opposite bank and the fleet anchored in 'Jyllingham waters'.

By the end of her reign **Upnor Castle** was as fit for the purpose as the technology could make it. It suffered minor tribulations during the Civil War, but it wasn't until 1667 that it was first put to the test for which it was built, and failed shamefully: a dishonour, wrote John Evelyn, that would never be wiped off. The Dutch sailed up the Medway on 12 June and, as Evelyn's fellow-diarist Samuel Pepys recorded, 'made no more of Upner castle's shooting then (*sic*) of a fly'. It transpired that the garrison had been cut the year before and besides was poorly supplied; by 30 June Pepys was writing: 'I do not see that Upnor Castle hath received any hurt by them [the Dutch], though they played long against it, and they themselfs [the English garrison] shot till they have hardly a gun left upon the carriages, so badly provided were they'.

Oldcastle and the Lollards
Shakespeare's Falstaff – vain, cowardly, flamboyant, 'fat-witted, with drinking of old sack', and who sold his soul to the devil 'for a cup of Madeira and a cold capon's leg' – was based on a man who seems to have had almost the opposite characteristics. It is true that Sir John Oldcastle, lord of Cooling Castle and Cobham manor in Kent, became a friend of the Prince of Wales. But Oldcastle was a man of deep seriousness, and became one of the most important followers of John Wycliffe. The latter attacked such church practices and beliefs as priestly indulgences and absolution, transubstantiation, and confession. His followers became known as Lollards (mutterers), and Oldcastle's position made him a natural leader of the heretical group. When Prince Hal became Henry V, Sir John is said to have tried to convert the king to his views. The two quarrelled and in 1414 a Lollard plot against the king was discovered and put down; Oldcastle was eventually captured and accused of planning to kill the king and make himself regent. He was executed in 1417. Lollardism lingered on and became absorbed into the widening stream of protestantism before, under Henry VIII, Wycliffe's 'heresies' became articles of the state-approved true faith.

Kent's Defences
The medieval castles of
Kent are testimony to the *ad
hoc* way in which defence
against an enemy, usually
the French, was organised
in the Middle Ages. After
the Romans, the first
systematic coastal defences
other than the loose alliance
of the Cinque Ports were
organised by Henry VIII
and Elizabeth I, not
surprisingly because after
their political break with
Rome troubles came 'not in
single spies, but in
batallions'. Henry built a
chain of forts along the
coast from Essex to
Cornwall, as has often been
said, in the shape of a
Tudor rose. But the shape
was functional, not
decorative, and was
designed to provide fields
of raking fire. The four in
Kent were Sandown, Deal,
Walmer and Sandgate.
Elizabeth's main
fortifications were to the
Thames and Medway
estuaries, and particularly
the series of forts
culminating in Upnor and
intended to protect
Chatham dockyards.
During the Napoleonic
wars the government
strengthened Dover Castle,
created the series of
fortifications above and
below ground on the
Western Heights above
Dover, built the chain of
Martello towers along the
coast (the pill boxes of their
time, each designed to
accommodate 22 soldiers),
and excavated the Royal
Military Canal between
Hythe and Rye. The battle
of Trafalgar rendered all
these preparations
redundant.

This seems to have been the general
conclusion, because apart from an increase in
the height of Upnor Castle no changes were
made and today Upnor looks much as it did at
the end of the 17th century. Instead the
Medway's defences were strengthened by the
addition of half a dozen other small forts and
batteries. But the Medway has never since
been so directly tested.

It takes an effort standing on the castle's
gun platform now to imagine the dismay that
Pepys felt, to the extent that he sent his wife
and father to the country with £1300 in gold.
Upnor is pretty in its ragstone and brick
neatness: turrets, a square gatehouse, gunports
and loops facing towards the water, mullioned
windows and roundels, timber palissades, all
built round a neat lawn with two tall turkey
oaks grown, it is said, from acorns brought
back from the Crimean War.

THE ISLE OF SHEPPEY

As you drive south towards the Swale under a
low, rain-charged sky, it could almost be
northern moorland. But here the long-ago
marshes have been drained and the channels
that did the work double up for irrigation.
Sheppey means 'isle of sheep', but now most
of the old pastures are under the plough.
South of the lane are Elmley Marshes, where
thousands of ducks, geese and waders spend
the winter and the RSPB has a reserve. At the
end of the lane is **Harty**, properly the Isle of
Harty, just about an island off an island, split
from the rest of Sheppey by Capel Fleet. Now
it is almost nothing: an inn where the ferry used
to ply to the mainland north of Faversham, a
couple of houses and a church, though once
there was a great house, Sayes Court. The
church is the reason why occasionally drivers
have to give way to each other in this remote
spot.

The churchyard of St Thomas overlooks the

Swale, which at this point is more than a ½-mile wide and dotted with pleasure craft and the occasional hoy (Kingsferry Bridge, which is the only land-route on to Sheppey, crosses a stretch of water no more than 150yds wide). There is a little shingled bellcote, sustained inside by massive 15th-century timbers; and there are three handsome kingposts through the remaining length of the church; but mainly the building is 11th and 12th century with a couple of Perpendicular windows and a lovely Decorated niche in the east wall of the chancel. Electricity and gas haven't reached this far, and the church is still lit by paraffin lamps. There is a tiny south transept that acts as a separate chapel, a north aisle of around 1200, and a simple and unspoilt 14th-century rood screen separating nave from chancel and north aisle from north chapel as well. For all its isolation, services still take place at St Thomas, on the first Sunday each month.

Back at the junction with the only east-west road on Sheppey, the B2231, the right leads to **Leysdown**, an immensely popular resort with a holiday population of caravan dwellers, and **Warden Point**, where bungalows periodically fall off the cliff into the sea. To the left is the road through Eastchurch and north-west to the highest point, geographically and spiritually, on the island. Here Queen Sexburga, wife of the grandson of England's first Christian king, Ethelbert, founded the abbey of **Minster** (Latin: *monasterium*) and herself became the first abbess in 670. The abbey itself went the way of all monasteries under Henry VIII, but the gatehouse survives, handsomely, and so does the abbey church of SS Mary and Sexburga.

On the approach, the church looks curiously like two adjoining churches: what you see is the nave of the abbey church with a rood screen dividing it from a chancel that has been rededicated as a chapel to St Sexburga (as she

Minster

S·SEXBVRGA·

Strange Pronunciations
England is notorious for the unstable connection between the spelling of place names and their pronunciations. Kent has more than its share of unphonetically spelt places. Here is a selection of booby traps for the unwary (pronunciation in brackets):

Barfreston (Barson); Boughton Aluph (Bawton); Boughton Malherbe (Bawton Mallaby); East and West Malling (Mawling); Elham (Eel-um); Eynsford (Aynsford); Eythorne (Aythorne); Great Mongeham (Mong-um); Horsmonden (Horsmonden: pronounced like most of the dens with the accent on the last syllable); Ightham (Eye-tum); Iwade (Eye-wade); Leigh (Lie); Lower and Upper Hardres (Hards); Lympne (Lim); Mereworth (Merryworth); Mersham (Merz-um); Teston (Teeson); Teynham (Tan-um); Tonbridge (Tunbridge, like the Wells and, indeed, its own original spelling); Trottiscliffe (Trosley: the authorities braved local contempt by spelling the country park above the village the way it is said); Wrotham (Root-um).

became); and the southern nave, the church built for the parishioners of Minister. The doorway within the south porch is Norman. There are Saxon windows very high up in the wall dividing the nun's church from the people's church, in St Sexburga's chapel there is an eastern wall with the marks of a reredos inside and out; and there are two fine brasses and three impressive monuments to knights of Sheppey. In the Minster gatehouse is an unusual museum of wirelesses and other vintage equipment, including early valve sets. It also has sweeping views of the Thames Estuary. The tower was being rebuilt in 1536 when Henry VIII made Minster Abbey one of his first targets, and building stopped halfway, leaving it now capped by a funny little shingled spire.

Queenborough is at the south-west of the island. Edward III built a fort here in 1361 and named it for his queen, Philippa of Hainault. Nothing of this remains, but there are Georgian houses in the attractive High Street running down to the water. A couple of miles further north is **Sheerness**, formerly a garrison town and Admiralty dockyard (commercial since 1960) of an importance in Kent second only to Chatham. Pepys helped to plan the dockyard in 1665 ('a most proper place it is for the purpose,' he wrote). The town still bustles with activity and seems somehow bigger than it actually is (about 15000 people). It is also very rundown. The handsome buildings at the entrance to the docks, Naval Terrace, still hang on to their Georgian dignity, but the big garrison church built in 1828 with a high and wide portico supported on Ionic columns is boarded up and the churchyard is choked with weeds. The noticeboards simply announce the prohibition of almost anything in the docks area, principally the entry of dogs or humans, the latter because there are many bonded warehouses within.

3 West Kent

Edenbridge was Eadhelm's bridge, so the name of the River Eden is a later derivation of the name of the town. No matter; most people consider the Eden happily named. This stretch of countryside, east from the Surrey border and south from the highest chalk slope in the county, Westerham Hill, is full of woods and water, small villages, big village greens with little cricket pavilions, narrow lanes lost and winding through the remains of medieval hunting forest, castles and moated and fortified granges. North of Sevenoaks, Holmdale, the valley beneath the chalk, meets the Darent (or Darenth), cutting across the grain of the country to head northwards toward the Thames. Nothing more sinister happens in this stretch of Kent than picnics by the Eden's side and paddling in the Darent, but the fortifications, from little Old Soar to Hever to the great gatehouse of Tonbridge Castle and the curtain wall of Eynsford are the beached remains of a troubled history.

Knole House

Sevenoaks

Population: 24,588

Market Day: Wed

Cashpoints: *Barclays* 80 High St; *Lloyds* 83 High St; *Midland* 69 High St; *Nat West* 67 High St, 138 High St

Tourist Information: Buckhurst Lane

Attractions: Ightham Mote, Knole*, Riverhill House*

Arts: The Stag Theatre

Leisure: Sevenoaks Swimming Pool, Wildernesse Sports Centre

By Road: London 26 miles (A224), Maidstone 18 miles (A25)

By Rail: 30mins from London (London, Charing Cross to Tonbridge line). Direct services to Ashford and Tunbridge Wells. Connections to Maidstone via Otford

SEVENOAKS

The most famous thing currently about **Sevenoaks** is that six of the seven oaks for which it is named blew down in the hurricane of 1987. Perhaps the town's name should revert to Sennock, by which it was anciently known. At any rate, the writer William Lambarde, whose *A Perambulation of Kent* (published 1575) is England's first county guide, treated the new name with great reserve, heading the chapter on the town, 'Sennocke, or (as some call it) Seven oke, of a number of trees, as they coniecture'.

Sevenoaks (to adapt Malcolm Muggeridge's acid phrase about a television personality) rose without trace. Lambarde was constrained to write:

I find not in all historie, any memorable thing concerning it, save onely, that in the time of King Henrie the sixt, Jack Cade, and his mischievous meiny, discomfited there Sir Humfrey Stafford, and his Brother, two Noble Gentlemen, whom the King had sent to encounter them.

Which qualifies as an early example of English understatement: Sir Humphrey and 24 of his men were killed.

It was and is a prosperous town. The arrival in 1868 of the Lewisham and Tonbridge branch of the London, Chatham and Dover Railway meant that Sevenoaks was now accessible to businessmen travelling day return to London. The population grew and with it the town spread, northwards as far as the Bat and Ball and south to the greensand ridge above Sevenoaks Weald, burying beneath neat villas the scene of Jack Cade's triumph. Today Sevenoaks is a busy country town and popular shopping centre, and its station is spankingly painted for the morning rush to London. In its early days Sevenoaks grew up along with its great house, Knole, whose family, the Sackvilles, first earls and then dukes of Dorset, gave the Vines to the town in 1773 to be a cricket ground in perpetuity. To this day flannelled fools – and others – perform rites more than two centuries old on the ground with its pretty white early-19th century pavilion. Most of what is worth seeing in Sevenoaks lies between the cricket ground and Sevenoaks School along the High Street.

The street is flanked by grand houses and tile-hung cottages: a tiny post office that bids to be the prettiest in England, a seven-bay mansion, Restoration houses (William and Mary), a Regency pub (the Royal Oak, with Tuscan columns supporting a porch and contemporary iron scroll balcony), plain doorcases and extravagant doorcases, and crisp white cornices. At the south-east of the street is the unforgiving grey ragstone front of Sevenoaks School, designed by Lord Burlington, patron of William Kent and himself a brilliant Palladian architect. Lord Burlington's design incorporates almshouses. When it was founded in 1418 by Sir William it was for the sons of the poor; now the school is for the clever, or for the sons and daughters of those who can afford it.

On the other side of the street is St Nicholas's Church, where a memorial tablet commemorates John Donne, who died here in 1631 after 15 years as rector: his poetry is too inward-looking to have any trace of Sevenoaks about it. Lambarde too has a memorial here. And on the east chancel wall of St Nicholas, almost opposite the entrance to Knole across the High Street, is inscribed:

To the Memory of John Braithwait Chief Coachman to his Grace Lionel Duke of Dorset He died by an unfortunate fall from his Coach near Riverhead in this parish. His loss was Greatly lamented by none more than by his Lord and Master to whom he was a most just and faithful servant.

The discreet entrance and narrow lane

William Lambarde

A Perambulation of Kent, by William Lambarde, is not so much a guide book, more a perambulation through history. It is the first history ever written of Kent. Lambarde was born in 1536. He inherited the family seat of Westcombe Manor, Greenwich (which in the 16th century was part of Kent) and lived there most of his life. He wrote the *Perambulation* in 1570, and in the same year married Jane Multon of Ightham. Her monument can be seen in the church: she died in 1573. Lambarde's second wife was Sylvestre Dalish, a wealthy widow of Halling. They lived at Halling Palace, part of one wall of which remains in Halling churchyard, and Sylvestre's monument is in the church. As justice of the peace for Kent, Lambarde wrote *The Office of the Justices of Peace*, which became the standard work for many years. In 1601 Queen Elizabeth personally appointed him to be keeper of the records at the Tower of London. He died later that year, but not before compiling an account of the records for the monarch. He was buried in St Alphege's church, Greenwich. When it collapsed in 1710, his relatives, who had moved to Sevenoaks, had his monument re-erected in Sevenoaks church. The *Perambulation* remains the best known of the many books he wrote, an entertaining volume full of sturdy Protestant opinion, classical allusion, quaint myth and scholarship.

Vineyards

Writing in 731, the Venerable Bede observed: 'Britain is rich in grain and timber; it has good pasturage for cattle and draught animals, and vines are cultivated in various localities'. But when Henry II married Eleanor of Aquitaine the vineyards of Bordeaux were part of her dowry and viticulture in England became a lost art. After World War II a growing group of enthusiasts began to think that if great wines could be grown in Germany, then so they could in the southern counties of England. Now English wines, with Kent and Sussex predominating, are shaking off the reputation of 'British wine', that appallingly sugary confection from foreign grape must. Predominantly light, white, crisp and fruity, Kentish wines win international blind tasting competitions and are served at banquets in Buckingham Palace and 10 Downing Street. Most vineyards are open to visitors and have wine tasting, often free, sometimes charged for. They include Bardingley (near Staplehurst), Biddenden, Chiddingstone, Conghurst (Hawkhurst), Elham Valley (Barham), Harbledown and Chaucer, Lamberhurst, Penshurst, St Nicholas of Ash (Ash-by-Sandwich), Staple, Tenterden, and Three Corners (Woodnesborough). By far the biggest is Lamberhurst, with 55 acres under vine.

leading from Sevenoaks High Street to **Knole House** and park are totally illusory. For the park that opens out beyond covers 1000 acres with a circumference of 6 miles. Within that boundary are a rose, shrub and herb garden, a golf course and a deer park. The fallow deer are comparatively tame, moving gracefully among parked cars, gently skirting excited children. In the more wooded areas are the smaller, shyer, sika deer. The landscape character of the park developed slowly over four centuries, until the hurricane of 1987 savagely re-arranged some of its more formal features with the violent felling of oak, beech and chestnut plantings.

From almost anywhere in the park Knole House looks like one of those small towns in a medieval book of hours. It is a big house, part medieval, part Tudor, part Jacobean, easiest to comprehend as built around three main quadrangles: the Green Court, the Stone Court and the Water Court. According to Vita Sackville-West, who was born and brought up there and should know, the legend is that 'its 7 courtyards correspond to the days of the week, its 52 staircases to the weeks of the year, its 365 rooms to the days of the year'.

Thomas Bourchier, Archbishop of Canterbury, bought the little manor house on a knoll outside Sevenoaks for £266 13s 4d in 1456 and transformed it from a pumpkin to a golden coach. By succession, it reached Archbishop Cranmer, but when the ever-avaricious Henry VIII came to visit he wrested it as a gift from the reluctant prelate, remarking, 'it standeth on a sound, perfect, and wholesome ground; and if I should make abode here, as I do surely mind to do now and then, I will live at Knole and most of my house shall live at Otford'. This was, in the king's way, a joke against Cranmer, who had also owned Otford until Henry relieved him of the trouble and expense.

At this time, the west front of Knole was

the front of the Stone Court. The king now
created the Green Court within more ranges of
buildings and a new west front and gatehouse.
Queen Elizabeth granted the house first to her
favourite, the Earl of Leicester, and then to the
Sackvilles. As soon as he gained full
possession of the house in 1603 Thomas
Sackville, first Earl of Dorset, made his mark.
He built the gables along the west and south
fronts with the Sackville leopard standing
proud at the top of each. He brought in 'the
king's plaisterer' to mould some of the
ceilings. The king's master carpenter,
William Portinton, carved the ornate screen in
the great hall and the exquisite oak panelling
painted ivory white in the ballroom. The Earl
had other rooms panelled as well. In the well
of the great staircase he had painted in greys
and greenish yellows the Four Ages of Man
and the Virtues and other allegories close
to his heart. On the banister he had carved
the proud Sackville leopard motif, and little
pieces of glass coloured with the Sackville
arms were set in the windows. In the ballroom
and the crimson drawing room he installed
two Jacobean Renaissance masterpieces
of sculpture, and the carved marble
fireplaces.

Through the rest of that century and the
next Thomas Sackville's descendants enriched
the house with acquisitions. The spendthrift
3rd Earl commissioned a lifesize sculpture,
displayed at the foot of the great staircase, of
the nude Giannetta Baccelli, his mistress. The
4th Earl filled the brown gallery with portraits
of historical figures. (Horace Walpole, who had
an eye for these things, remarked: 'They seem
to have been bespoke by the yard, and drawn
all by the same painter'.) The William III
furniture was introduced by the 6th Earl, 'the
grace of courts, the muses' pride', in Dryden's
phrase, who as Chamberlain to the royal
household had the right to take for himself

items that had fallen out of fashion. By this perquisite he brought to Knole Brussels tapestries for the spangle bedroom, the early-17th-century furniture in the Leicester Gallery, and the bed made for James II, redundant when he fled the country, and now in the Venetian Ambassador's room. The 6th Earl brought to Knole the studio of Mytens's copies of the Raphael cartoons. He also received, in what would now be vulgarly recognised as bribery, the gift from Louis XIV of the gilt table and candlestands in the crimson drawing room after the successful conclusion of the infamous secret treaty of Dover, by which Charles II promised to turn apostate in return for French help against the Dutch.

Best of all is last of all: the Louis XIV bed in the king's room made for James II, then Duke of York, to celebrate his marriage to Mary of Modena, its feet carved with lions, its woodwork gilt and silver, its canopy gold and silver – the thread painstakingly restored over the last few years; and the silver furniture and dressing table accessories, not indeed unique, because there is some similar at Windsor, but matchless for its grandiloquent expression of luxury at any price, all late-17th and early-18th-century English and French.

The contents of most of the house are viewed in light filtered through fine gauze; in the king's room the treasures are behind glass as well. The effect is to heighten the sense of a great medieval, Tudor, and Stuart household locked in a time warp. Sackvilles still live here, in rooms not normally open to the public, but the rest is administered by the National Trust.

East of Sevenoaks is **Seal**, with its attractive woods to the south as far as the ragstone ridge. The village is a posh adjunct to Sevenoaks, with a lot of big suburban houses; but although it is sundered by the A25, Seal is still pleasant.

Beyond Seal is **Ightham**, which to most

people, is the Mote. But the Mote is a couple of miles away, and the village asserts its own personality. The George and Dragon and a few other houses in its vicinity form a group that is an archetype of half-timbered Kentish vernacular building, and the churchyard looks west over neat little orchards towards heavily wooded hills. One of the hills is Oldbury, the site of a 2nd century BC fort, captured in the 1st century by the Belgae, incomers from France, and reduced to ashes by Claudius.

Apart from Ightham Mote, there is another manor house, north of the A25. This is **Ightham Court**, a 16th-century brick building with a little clock tower sitting in a meadow above the railway line through Borough Green: a daily treat for commuters.

Ightham church is above the village and the approach is through a pretty lychgate. There are two attenuated aisles, the northern one brick built as late as the 17th century. The outstanding thing, however, is the sheer weight of monumental sculpture in the little chancel. In the south-aisle chapel are memorials to not just one, but two Ightham holders of the Victoria Cross for extreme gallantry.

In the chapel at **Ightham Mote** is another memorial to the gallant Lieutenant Colyer-Ferguson VC. Actually, there are two chapels: extraordinary in a small manor house, but then this is an extraordinary house. It is found (with less difficulty since the useful brown signposts were erected) down a warren of narrow lanes in heavily wooded country. It is a beautiful medieval house of the 14th century, very nearly complete, and what is not complete the National Trust is doing its best to restore. It is no bigger than a large family house but it has a moat, with goldfish and ducks, a 15th- to 16th-century gatehouse with a stone slit beside it for challenging strangers, and a courtyard with the great hall of the house facing the gatehouse.

Ightham Mote

Mostly it is built of ragstone, but its 16th-century owners, the Clements, built ranges of half-timbering; one of them is the second chapel.

The hall has practically the proportions of a gatehouse itself, and the impression is confirmed inside, for it is higher (37ft) than it is long or wide, and a massive five-light Perpendicular window fills the West wall with glass emblazoned with the Tudor rose, the pomegranate of Katherine of Aragon, and Henry VIII's personal emblem, the portcullis. The fireplace is 16th-century as well, with an iron fireback dated 1583 which must have been cast in one of the foundries of the Weald. The timber roof is carried on corbels carved with the figures of peasants cheerfully bearing their burden through the ages.

Plaxtol

Close by, the 14th-century rib-vaulted crypt with a Decorated window only just above the water level of the moat carries the weight of the original chapel above, and which itself (reached by a Jacobean wooden staircase) was adapted into living quarters when Sir Richard built what is now known as the Tudor Chapel. The solar, or upper living room, is 16th century, and has fine timber rafters and a crown post and a beautiful timber oriel window. The other half of the solar was converted into a bedroom and bathroom during the 19th century and is being put back into its original condition by the National Trust.

Beyond this is the 16th-century chapel, with lovely linenfold panelling at the east end and a barrel-vaulted wagon ceiling bearing, like the window in the great hall, the motifs of the Tudors and Aragons, the paint faded now, but still resonant as the banners and kettledrums of the Field of the Cloth of Gold. And beyond the chapel in the north-west corner of the house is the drawing room, with a lavish part-Renaissance wholly Jacobean fireplace carved with the arms of the Selbys, who owned the house in the 17th century, and with portrait busts which might, at a guess, be Sir William and Lady Selby. There is an old and charming garden, and there are stories: the skeleton of a young woman found behind a wall, and the rumour that Dame Dorothy Selby betrayed the Gunpowder Plot. Most romantic of all is the story of Charles Henry Robinson of Portland, Maine, who fell in love with a picture of the Mote when a young man. The chance to buy it came many years later, and he lavished care on it until his death in 1985. He never married: the house was his abiding passion. His ashes are in the crypt.

A carved stone above the door inside the porch of **Plaxtol** church says baldly: 'This church was built for the worship of God anno domini 1649'. Its erection was ordered by Archbishop Laud but it was finished during the Commonwealth and would have been the only complete Cromwellian church in Kent had the Victorians left well alone. They didn't; and to compound the felony the *Luftwaffe* dropped a bomb on the church. Still, the austere nave remains completely of 1649.

The best things are all wooden: the hammer-beam rafters, the 17th-century reredos in the south transept chapel depicting a headless but dominating Moses ordering the parting of the Red Sea for his followers, the Jacobean pulpit with wild-eyed baroque prophets taken from somewhere else and gummed uneasily across the panels of the pulpit, and the wooden carvings within the stone reredos of the high altar. In the West Kent volume of *The Buildings of England*, John Newman deduces that these are 15th-century Flemish, which means around the time of the Van Eycks. They are certainly beautiful representations of the crucifixion, the deposition, and the entombment with little woods and towns on rocky hills in the background.

The village is a lovely mixture of domestic

The Kingdom of Kent
Kent was once a kingdom in its own right; the modern boundaries describe, nearly enough, the boundaries of the post-Roman kingdom. In AD 455 the Continental leaders, Hengist and Horsa, fought a decisive battle as mercenaries against the Saxons on behalf of the British leader Vortigern at Aylesford. They took Thanet as their reward, and were followed by other settlers spreading across Kent from Jutland and the Frankish middle Rhine. Four decades after the battle at Aylesford, Aesc, a direct descendant of Hengist, or so he claimed, became the first in a royal line. It lasted, with short intervals when the kings of Mercia and Wessex assumed suzerainty, until 825, the year when Kent submitted to King Egbert of Wessex and ceased for ever to be a separate kingdom.

The best-known of this royal line was King Ethelbert, who ruled from 560 until his death in 616. He is famous not only because he received St Augustine at his court and eventually embraced Christianity on his own and his kingdom's behalf, but because he was the first king in England to enact and publish a series of new laws, including a scale of damages for personal injuries (6s for a broken arm, 50s for the loss of an eye), an exemption from taxes for the church, and a system for pursuing lawsuits.

Bricks and stones
Brick and tile is
characteristic of Kent.
North of Maidstone the
lime content of gault clay
yields pale yellow brick
(known as whites); alluvial
earths in North Kent give
deep browns; in the
Malling area iron in the
earth gives plummy reds
and sloe blues, and in the
Weald soft glowing
oranges. Tile-hanging, like
weatherboarding, is a
device to protect houses
against driving rain. Often
brick and tile disguise much
older timber-framed houses
beneath.

Along with the Weald,
the gault, and the alluvial
brick-yielding clays, three
more main geological strata
run parallel across Kent
from the Surrey border to
the English Channel
roughly east-south-east.
Beautiful sandstones are
typical in the Weald. The
greensand hills yield
Kentish rag, a rough
limestone very typical of
the area, and floated by the
Romans on barges to
London for the city wall,
and later by the Victorians
for many of the churches.
Whenever fine detail was
needed, the medieval
builders brought stone from
Caen, Normandy, and in
the case of a major
building, like Canterbury
Cathedral, the whole edifice
would be of Caen stone.
Bethersden marble (really a
freshwater limestone full of
molluscs which polishes to
a beautiful grey) can be
seen at its best in a
memorial at Chilham, and
two gorgeous fireplaces at
Godinton Park.

brick, tile and weatherboard. One much-
capped England goalkeeper always came on a
pilgrimage here whenever he was playing
within reach (maybe still does) – for the local
butcher's herb-flavoured pork sausages. But
the best reason for visiting Plaxtol lies down an
obscure lane a mile or so north-east. **Old Soar**
is remarkable even in a county in which the
Royal Commission on the Historical
Monuments of England estimates there may be
as many as 4000 medieval houses hiding
behind later disguises. Old Soar is the solar,
chapel, lavatorium, and barrel-vaulted
undercroft – impressively intact structurally
and with tremendous collar beams and king
posts – of a manor house of 1290, built by the
great Kentish family, the Culpeppers.
Paradoxically, whereas a timber and wattle and
daub structure could be adapted easily to
changing conditions and new notions of
comfort, stone could not. So the great hall was
demolished in place of the lovely though far
from unique Georgian red-brick farmhouse
beside Old Soar, but the solar wing survived
because it was useful as a barn. There are big
fine Gothic windows at each end of the
building.

The entrance is through the undercroft and
up a clockwise spiral staircase. The rooms are
on the first floor, probably as a precaution
against damp, vermin and wandering outlaws.
These were not easy times. An ancient oak
door displayed in the solar has period doodling
incised on it: one figure of an armed fighting
man, and several of corpses suspended from
gibbets. The chapel, which enabled the
Culpeppers to worship at home instead of
riding to Wrotham, nearly 5 miles away, is half
the size of the living room and has a fine
cinquefoil-headed piscina.

All that existed of Plaxtol at the time was a
chapel where the church stands now. From the
lie of the land it is easy to see how central Old

Soar was to this stretch of countryside. The lanes are the same, though metalled; field patterns have not changed much in the intervening centuries, though planting has moved from subsistence wheat and beans to cash crops of apples, pears, broccoli, potatoes and hops. In the chamber beneath the solar, English Heritage has mounted an exemplary display of imaginative and well-researched information setting Old Soar and its lord in their context, national and local.

Up a little road off the A227 and signposted to West Peckham, **Shipbourne** has a house built by the Bauhaus master, Walter Gropius, in 1937. It is called the Wood House and is faced in weatherboarding. For all the apparent attempt to fit in with the Kentish vernacular, the house is more in an international style than Kentish. Gropius left for the USA before the work was over and Maxwell Fry finished it for him; Eric Lyons in turn was a pupil of Maxwell Fry, and at *New Ash Green* 30 years later Lyons adapted the Gropius approach to a large tract of North Downs countryside.

General Wolfe, born in Westerham

South of Shipbourne is Great Hollanden Farm which is now home to various rare breeds of farm animals. A little to the west, on **Riverhill**, is Riverhill House. It has been owned by the same family for close on 150 years and the garden reflects generations of love and care. The garden was one of the first to be opened under the National Gardens Scheme when it was set up in 1927. It deserves to be better known and undoubtedly would be, were it not in a county blessed with many fine gardens.

Westerham's two heroes, Wolfe of Quebec and Churchill of Chartwell, dominate the village green, Wolfe's leaden (the material, not the effect) statue flourishing an imperious sword; Churchill's sitting hunched. Unfortunately, while Oscar Nemon saw Winston as powerfully brooding, the effect of his sculpture is merely lumpen. But children find it friendly and climb on it as though it were a favourite grandfather.

The green is a big triangle and gives the small town breathing space from the press of traffic on the A25. It is a bustling little place, and the fine houses are mixed with the ordinary in a welcoming ensemble. Wolfe was born in the vicarage but spent his childhood in a multi-gabled Jacobean house at the bottom of the hill approaching the town, the Spiers, now Quebec House and run by the National Trust as a Wolfe museum. Wolfe received his first commission, at the age of 14, at Squerryes Court, a fine 17th-century house looking over a lake. The Darent rises in the grounds of the house. Westerham's church sits as four-square on its little hill above the green as Sir Winston on his bronze chair. Within, there are very early royal arms for the short-lived Edward VI, Elizabeth I's younger brother and predecessor on the throne.

Strictly speaking **Chartwell** is part of Crockham Hill (home of Octavia Hill, co-founder of the National Trust), but everyone looks for it from Westerham. It lies spectacularly on the greensand ridge a couple of miles to the south. When Winston Churchill bought the house in 1922 it was only one room thick. His architect added rooms and a terrace at the back, the dining room with Lady Churchill's bedroom above. The National Trust have turned part of the house into a Winston museum: his uniforms, the Garter, the hats; the Boer war poster offering a reward for the young Winston dead or alive; the gifts given to him by his peers, Stalin and Roosevelt; and photographs of his great meetings. But essentially the house is Lady Churchill's: chintzy, comfortable, easy, just the place for a great statesman to glower through the windows along the combe above which Chartwell is built. For this above all was the

Winston Churchill,
owner of Chartwell

house of his retirement and, during the 1930s, of his years in the wilderness waiting for the call. Sir Winston wrote sonorously of himself in *The Gathering Storm*, 'I never had a dull or idle moment from morning till midnight, and with my happy family around me dwelt at peace within my habitation'. The contented Winston, neglected by his nation but peaceful in the bosom of his family: it must be one of the great fictions.

There are many paintings of Churchill in the house, and of his parents. There are respectable pictures by artists like Lavery and Sargent, and one great painting, a view of the Thames by Monet, sufficient to have put a shrinking violet off painting for life. Not, of course, Sir Winston. He painted and painted, often badly even for an amateur, but always boldly and sometimes well, and his garden studio is lined with his paintings, finished and unfinished, with one on the easel waiting for its finishing touches, paintbox near to hand. Churchill threw himself into work around the grounds, building great garden walls, excavating a swimming pool and ponds for the golden orfe to bask – the bench where he sat beside the pond and the box from which he fed the fish are still there. Above all, there are those tremendous views across the Weald, Hastings beyond and beyond that the Channel, and France . . . but in the war years, of course, Winston was more likely to be found in the bunker beneath the Admiralty with no view beyond the charts on the wall.

Chevening is a village living in the shadow of the glory of its great house in beautiful parkland on the scarp slope of the North Downs. The house was built in the time of Charles I and no less than Colen Campbell, architect of Mereworth Castle, ascribes it to Inigo Jones. It can only be seen through trees from footpaths below Knockholt (whose own

King Cnut
The men in longboats who visited fire and destruction upon these shores between the departure of the Romans and the coming of the Normans often arrived as raiders and stayed as kings. Such was Swein, King of Denmark, and such a one was his son, Cnut (around 994–1035). For all their disorderly ways, they did not simply arrive at any convenient beach: Swein and his son particularly made it a practise to sail into port at Sandwich. In 1013 Swein swept through Kent and Wessex, King Ethelred fled to Normandy, and Swein was proclaimed in his stead. But he died the same year and Cnut sailed for Denmark, leaving behind at Sandwich the hostages rendered to his father, minus their noses, ears and hands. He had been born pagan, and though now baptised with the name Lambert his notion of Christian humility was rudimentary. The following year he returned, again through Sandwich, and although his Danes lost a battle against Ethelred's son, Edmund Ironside, at Otford, Edmund died soon after and Cnut was proclaimed king. He ruled until his death, surrounded by Christian scholars, dispensing justice under laws written for him by the Archbishop of York, and celebrated in song as 'Gracious Giver of Mighty Gifts'. One gift to the monks of Christ Church, Canterbury, was the right to collect tolls from the ferry across the Stour.

The Pilgrims' Way

The Pilgrims' Way is older than pilgrims; older even than most of the settlements it passes by. It was first called the Pilgrims' Way on the 19th-century Ordnance Survey maps, but the route was used in prehistoric times. Unlike prehistoric routes on the more fertile land below, it has not been obscured by later developments. Originally it linked the Continent through Straits of Dover to the important centres of Avebury and Stonehenge, where six early highways converged. It remained a popular route to the West even after the Romans built Watling Street to London; and because the Archbishops of Canterbury built their palaces along the way, it remained a royal route to the Channel ports, most famously for Henry VIII on his way to Dover. Later, it became a way of avoiding tolls on the turnpikes. The modern name is misleading: pilgrims from London went to Canterbury along the route of the present A2. For those that did use the Way, churches at Snodland and Burham (on each side of the Medway) provided accommodation. Today the Pilgrims' Way runs 120 miles between Winchester and Canterbury. Together with its companion North Downs Way it provides some of the loveliest walking country in the south of England.

high beeches are said to be visible from Harrow on the Hill), but it is a stirring sight. The gardens are splendid too.

Below the village on the A25 are **Brasted** and **Sundridge**, both with many fine houses but suffering, despite the M25, from the traffic on the A25. Brasted Place, now a training college, is a magnificent Robert Adam mansion with a bizarre 19th-century extension. Napoleon III stayed there, restlessly walking the grounds with his tame eagle, before returning to Paris as Emperor.

Ide Hill is a tiny village standing round a sloping green up a steep hill leading from Sundridge. Above the green is the church, standing on the edge of the Greensand Ridge. Beside the church is a footpath which looks like a private drive and leads into National Trust territory and some of the most glorious views in England. Ide Hill suffered in the 1987 hurricane but not to the extent of its neighbour to the west, **Toys Hill**. The wooded summit of Toys Hill with its delightful, enchanted glimpses of the Weald through the trees was obliterated in a matter of hours; a new path for disabled visitors became an obstacle course for the fittest. Toys Hill is heartbreaking, although the views of the Weald survive – different for our lifetime, but still superb. Down the hill is **Emmetts Garden**, a charming shrub garden also in the stewardship of the National Trust and also greatly damaged by the storm. At Emmetts the process of replacing plants beyond their prime had already begun; partly as a result of this the garden was rallying by the end of 1988.

THE DARENT VALLEY

North of Sevenoaks runs the Darent Valley, where the first village to stop at is **Otford**. Like Eynsford, unlike Shoreham and Farningham, Otford peace is disturbed by the traffic on the A225, which enters the village at the pond on the little green between the church and main street, and then loops around the modern, northern part of the village before following the line of the Darent northwards. The pond is unique, for it is the only area of water in England designated as a listed building – Friston pond in Sussex is an ancient monument. Otford pond was first recorded in the 11th century but it is really the containing walls which are the subject of the listing. The pond has its own keeper of wildlife to ensure that the ducks who add to the rural effect are content to remain. The village remains singularly rustic in the face of creeping urbanisation and its appearance belies its turbulent past. In 774 the army of King Offa of Mercia fought the army of King Aldric of Kent here; and in 1016 Edmund Ironside routed Cnut's Danes (futile, because Edmund died the same November and Cnut became king). Moreover, processions of royalty or churchmen from London would take ship at Greenwich or Dartford, turn south down the Darent, and at Otford meet the Old Road, or Pilgrims' Way as it is known today, and travel on to Canterbury or the coast. So the Archbishop of Canterbury built a mansion at Otford – Becket often stayed here. At the beginning of the 16th century Archbishop Warham turned it into a palace (to the disapproval of William Lambarde, who called it a monument to misbegotten treasure). Henry VIII, who travelled to France along the Pilgrims' Way for the meeting at the Field of the Cloth of Gold, took over the Otford palace from his archbishop, though soon he was complaining that it gave him rheumatism.

It was very big – built around two courtyards and 220ft wide in the west front, which made it not much smaller than Knole, though Knole is more than 400ft deep. After the king's death the palace became derelict and all that remains now is an octagonal tower and part of a gatehouse with the range between adapted into a row of cottages. The palace lies in a watermeadow along a footpath from the church of St Bartholomew. Among the miracles ascribed to Becket, was that he struck his staff into the ground east of the church to produce the palace's water supply ('the fraude of the Popish Priestes,' growled Lambarde).

Shoreham is the heart of Samuel Palmer's 'Valley of Vision'. Palmer, one of a group of followers of William Blake, first visited Shoreham in 1824. In 1827 he came to live in the neat, white, stuccoed Water House with the big old yew tree in the garden set back from the road and the little bridge over the Darent, and painted his remarkable visions of a paradise on earth, 'Dream of a dream, and shadow of a shade', in the words of Milton, whom he revered. This period lasted for a little less than eight years, and then the necessity to make a living drove him back to London and to a tour of Italy, where a combination of real life and a study of the High Renaissance masters watered down his own deeply personal response to the natural world.

He drew and painted all over the Darent Valley. Many of the studies are purely topographical: lovely views of Shoreham from the hills around, of Sepham barn (the barn has gone, the farm is still there halfway along the lane to Otford), and of the great trees in Lullingstone Park. On these he based the works on which his own fame is based, and a good deal of the fame of Shoreham. He painted trees like great mushrooms, clouds like gathered bunches of blossom, blossom like clotted cream: the whole sentient world became an expression of his feelings about life and after-life, and some of the paintings explicitly set biblical events, like the flight into Egypt, alongside this enchanted Darent. And yet the paintings remain recognisably the

Darent Valley, and it is difficult for anyone who has looked at the paintings to see Shoreham other than through Samuel Palmer's eyes.

The village has grown, of course, since Palmer's day, but not the centre, with the right-angled bend in the road at the foot of the hill just before the river, a variety of cottages and dignified Georgian houses, the 15th-century church with a well proportioned 18th-century red-brick tower with pinacles, and a pretty path running alongside willows by the river and through fields northwards to Lullingstone and Eynsford.

Lullingstone Park is 300 acres of natural woodland on the hill above Shoreham. Like all the high places of Kent it suffered in the hurricane of 1987, but it survives nobly. At the time of writing, the car park was fringed by a squalid tide line of litter; beyond that, this is a pleasant place, catering for golfers and people exercising the dog, and yet providing in Beechen Wood, south of the golf course, an excellent wilderness habitat for birds and plants. The path follows the line of a hedgerow at least 600 years old, with arable land on one side and the great oaks and beeches of the park on the other. There are long and short walks signposted and fine views of the tree-edged river and the hop gardens and orchards below.

Sir Derek Hart Dyke is only the 9th Baronet (created 1696), but his family have held the manor of Lullingstone by indirect descent for 600 years. So **Lullingstone Castle**, Queen Anne behind a gatehouse of 1497, is extraordinary. We expect to be impressed by the Hatfields, the Knoles, the Penshursts and the Hampton Courts. But from before the Reformation the gentry of England were the coming force, and then the families who made the history of England. The history of Lullingstone is the history of England writ small.

Watermills
Domesday records around 350 watermills in Kent, and at Ickham, east of Canterbury, there are the remains of two Roman watermills (only four others are known in Britain). At first the mills were used for grinding corn; they were a central part of the economy and were usually annexed to the lord of the manor's demesne. Fulling cloth (which involves forcing fulling earth, of which Kent has a good supply, through the weave of the cloth to carry away grease) gave a further impetus to watermills. The paper industry, introduced into England in the 16th century, gave another: a small hamlet like Mill Street in East Malling, which had two mills at the time of Domesday, had four in the 19th century. Even where mills stand on Domesday sites, the buildings themselves are mostly 16th- to 19th-century. Mills often performed more than one function; sometimes a mill would switch from milling corn to papermaking; and occasionally a mill that had been purpose-built for papermaking switched to milling corn. But better roads, better transport, a growing population and industrialisation spelt the end of the small miller. Where they have not been demolished or fallen down, a few mills have been maintained in working order or have been converted for other uses. At Swanton Mill, near Mersham, corn is ground and can be bought.

Fruit Growing

Pliny says that the Romans took cherry stock into Britain; by the 16th century William Lambarde was writing, 'As for orchards of apples, and gardens of cherries, and those of the most delicious and exquisite kinds that can be, no part of the realm (that I know) hat them either in such quantity and number, or with such art and industry set and planted'. Celia Fiennes reported travelling the Watling Street 'which is all by the side of Cherry grounds that are of severall acres of ground and runs quite down to the Thames'. The cherry orchards have all but disappeared, because cheap imports have made the problems of protecting the early blossom against frost and then the fruit against birds not worth the expense. Even the apple orchards are under threat from mass imports of Common Market fruit. But despite the warnings, the Kent fruit growing industry still flourishes with something like 50,000 acres growing the new dwarf variety of quick and heavy-yielding tree and bringing in its wake earnings from tourists anxious to see the spectacular spring blossom. The former East Malling Research Station, now the Institute of Horticultural Research, has pioneered the development of soft fruit in Britain. Many varieties have Malling in their names.

One lord of the Lullingstone manor, Sir John Peche, was champion of Henry VII's royal jousting tourney in 1494; another, Sir Percyval Hart, a survivor of the politics of the reigns of Henry VIII, Mary I, Edward VI, and Elizabeth I, died in his bed aged 84. A later Sir Percival Hart built the Queen Anne house (literally: she came to stay and it was to a degree designed to cater for her needs) and, though a Jacobite, served his queen because, presumably, as daughter of the deposed James II she was acceptable; but on the accession of George I Sir Percival retired to cultivate his garden. It is all here: the pragmatic marriage to the scion of an ironmaster, the career made at the bar or from the estates, the gentlemen of England, proud of their identity.

Their history can be read, literally and between the lines, in the inscriptions on the tombs in the church of St Botolph, a parish church of the Middle Ages but within the walls of Lullingstone Castle and rebuilt by the family, who have alabaster monuments there as splendid as the royal sepulchres of Westminster. The house itself and the grounds – where the Darent was dammed to create a waterfall, a weir, and a beautiful lake – carry everywhere the marks of pride.

In later years, it became known for the Lullingstone Silk Farm, which provided materials for princesses' dresses and World War II parachutes. The silk farm has moved to Dorset but kept the name.

Lullingstone Roman villa lies in the valley up by the clear waters of the river, an easy walk through the park. It is reached by car up a dead-end lane from Eynsford. Beneath a great shed designed to protect and allow in maximum light are the remarkable remains of a villa first built 30 or 40 years after the legions of Claudius established the Roman presence in Britain. There are the remains of baths, underfloor heating, living and dining rooms with fine mosaic floors (one depicting Europa and the Bull), a temple, and, highly unusual, the later addition of a Christian chapel with Chi Rho monograms. After various vicissitudes following the fluctuating fortunes of the Roman occupation, the villa burned down in the 4th century. The remains were covered and protected by a mudslip until it was excavated after World War II.

Eynsford straddles the A225 through Darent Valley. The church with its tall broach spire east of the road looks down the lane that leads to Lullingstone Roman villa, over a little 17th-century villa beside a ford at a point where the stream is so domesticated it becomes an integral part of the village, as much as the winding road, the pretty pub (The Plough), and the half-timbered houses. Just down from the ford in the 12th century William de Eynsford built a castle whose ruined curtain walls – a visual surprise in such a ducks-and-lily-pond sort of place – still stand as much as 30ft high. You can still see the remains of the castle hall and the ditch.

Church and castle were the focus of an early but key dispute between Henry II and Becket. The dispute was over who had the power to grant the living of Eynsford church. William de Eynsford turned down Becket's appointee on the grounds that the living had always been the gift of the Eynsford family; Becket maintained that church appointments should be in the hands of the Church. Henry II supported William; Becket excommunicated him, and so the die was cast for the quarrel between the two, a dispute over the competing powers of Church and State which came to a gory climax with the murder of Becket in Canterbury Cathedral in 1170.

The see of Canterbury announces its presence in the parish church, St Martin of Tours, with its arms alternating with the Tudor rose on the eight faces of the Perpendicular

font. Within the west porch is an inner
doorway, mid-12th century, pure Norman and
impressive as always: there is zig-zag
patterning on the arches and diaper patterning
in the tympanum and columns with scalloped
capitals. Best of all are the simple but effective
sculpted heads, sometimes as corbels,
sometimes simply growing out of the wall of
the church.

Farningham sits a few yards south of where
the A20 and M20 cut across the Darent Valley
in parallel. Bureaucratic ingenuity has ensured
that a huge signpost gantry stands on the hill
above the village in sight and out of scale with
everything below. Otherwise Farningham
remains one of the pearls strung along the
river.

The handsome Georgian Lion Hotel
dominates the approach from the road through
the valley, just over the brick bridge built 'by
order of the Court of Quarter Sessions' in 1773.
Once at the bridge the real treat is the big,
broad, white, weatherboarded mill behind a
manicured lawn and with a mill house as
extravagantly handsome as a regency beau (but
of an earlier period), and what at the time was
no doubt regarded as a modest cottage
guarding the gate, but to which the years have
lent enchantment.

The church is 13th century, fairly heavily
restored without, and within unremarkable
except for some of the detail: the piscina in the
chancel and a wall recess at the south-east of
the nave; but best of all a font carved on its
eight faces with the sacraments: a stone comic
strip of 15th-century costume, and carved with
just that kind of crude vitality.

North of the trunk roads of the M20 and
A20, the A225 beside the Darent turns into a
dreary stretch of building reaching a long
grubby finger as far as Dartford. A spectacular
railway viaduct signals the river's course, but
nothing in **Sutton-at-Hone** but a tiny National

Trust signpost half obscured by bushes indicates that here is the house and garden of **St John's Jerusalem** (look out for the agricultural equipment showroom of Ernest Doe: St John's is next door).

The approach is through a farm gate and over a field. St John's is within a willow-fringed square moat formed by the Darent. The house is 17th century, but the east wing contains the chapel of the original commandery. Robert de Basing, lord of the manor, gave his house to the new St John's order in 1199. Henry III, who reigned from 1216 to 1272, stayed here often and provided six great oaks for the building. The order was dissolved in 1540 and in the 17th century Abraham Hill, a founder of the Royal Society and introducer of the making of cider to Kent, rebuilt the house. Edward Hasted, the historian of Kent, lived here in the 18th century and went broke improving the house further. The National Trust has been having other problems but is busy now restoring the garden to its former glory.

It is, anyway, a place of peace, dignity and charm. The house stands behind a great cedar of Lebanon and a copper beech. Old roses grow round about, reeds edge the moat, and on the lawn grow horse chestnuts, sweet chestnuts, alder, elder, and big flowering cherry trees, with fig and magnolia growing against the south-facing wall of the house. The ragstone chapel has three lancet windows in the east wall and two in the south. Close by, and bounded now by the A20 and M20, is Brand's Hatch – no longer home to the British Grand Prix as a result of tensions between the various bodies who control the sport but an immensely exciting circuit for drivers and spectators alike. Set in a natural amphitheatre, it has been the scene of racing since the 1920s. The early events were motorbike races on grass, and car races did not begin until

Farningham Mill

after 1945 when a suitable surface had been put down.

WROTHAM AND THE NORTH DOWNS

The tungsten lights on the M20 have given **Wrotham** a night-time character over the last few years that it could have done without. Still, sandwiched as it is between motorway and bypass, Wrotham remains an archetypal English village, centred in a tiny area on church, manor house, square and High Street. The church was built in the 13th century and dedicated to St George before England took him as patron saint. There is a bronze of St George by Wili Soukop, the Royal Academician, in a small niche above the south porch – better than the bronze it replaced, which was stolen.

Perhaps the parish church owes its handsome size to the Archbishops of Canterbury, who not only owned this manor from the time of the Norman Conquest, but who had a palace here. It was demolished by Archbishop Islip late in the 14th century and the stone cannibalised for the new palace at Maidstone. There are remains behind the dignified Bull Inn. The church tower has an archway beneath it to enable sacred processions to move around the church without leaving sanctified ground. Inside is a 13th-century font with blind arcades incised on each of its eight sides; a 14th-century rood screen; and a turret with a stone newel staircase leading nowhere (it once led to the rood loft). Victorian angels support an ornately carved pulpit (the original Jacobean oak pulpit is now in Sevenoaks church; baddish luck on Wrotham), and a series of small brasses is spread out in the nave. The original mensa (stone top of the altar) was removed at the Reformation, but has been recovered and is cemented into the floor beneath the high altar.

The manor house is across the road from

the church, Elizabethan, but added to in the 19th century, the offices of a company now, but beautifully maintained with lawns and flowerbeds elegantly coiffured and some of the big lime trees that characterise the village. The High Street has several good Georgian houses.

To the west is **Kemsing** which lies criss-crossed by lanes meandering through beautiful countryside. It must be hard for train commuters to resist the urge to alight at Kemsing station, close to the pretty hamlet of **Heaverham**, and simply wander. Just below the North Downs Way at Heaverham lies St Clere, a fine coral red brick mansion of 1633. An earlier owner, born in the house, described it as having 'the fairest view in Kent'. The presence of the M26 has not improved the view but the house remains quite delightful. A short distance west along the North Downs Way, the Kent Trust for Nature Conservation have a reserve on the chalky scrub above Kemsing, where many species of lime-loving plants thrive and a good variety of butterflies can be found. Paths lead down from the reserve to the village which has grown considerably in recent years but the centre, around the church, is largely unaltered.

Wrotham Hill stands well over 500ft above sea level. I have driven down the A20 and seen a light aircraft flying below me. There is a view-point near the roundabout at the top of the hill with some of the finest views in Kent. **Ash-by-Wrotham** stands reluctantly close to its neighbour, **New Ash Green**, which was created starting in 1967 with a stroke of Richard Crossman's pen, overriding the housing ministry inspector's recommendations after a public planning inquiry. The Labour government didn't stick around long enough to see the eventual result of the plan. The village was designed and built by Eric Lyons and Span as a large-scale demonstration of how architect and builder could work together to build a modern village. The styles mixed modern and

Place Names
Very broadly, the early history of Kent can be told from its place names. The county itself dates back 8000 years to the point at which the sea broke through the marshy strip connecting the North Downs with the Pas de Calais and formed the straits of Dover. Cantus, to the British, meant edge. Julius Caesar adopted Cantium, and Canterbury takes its name from the county, though in earliest times it was known as Darovernon (adopted by the Romans as *Durovernum*).

British and Romans were superseded by Saxon and Jute, and it is Saxon names that dot the map of Kent. They resettled or rebuilt old British and Romano-British villages, starting in the river valleys and on the uplands. The oldest names have '-ing' endings, like Malling, Charing, Kemsing, denoting a tribal settlement (Malling: the place of Mealla's people); or their Saxon derivation may be buried deeper, as in Woodensborough (Woden's Hill); or they end in '-ham', meaning settlement: Faversham, Chatham, Lenham, Burham, Shoreham. Places incorporating Street into their names, like Green Street Green or Sole Street, refer to places which had the remains of paved Roman roads. Then there was the final flourish of Wealden clearances with place names ending in '-den' (woodland pasture), '-ley' or '-leigh' (clearing), or '-hurst' (wooded hill).

Eliza Acton
When Queen Adelaide visited Tonbridge after the death of her husband, William IV, in 1837, Eliza Acton presented her with some verses complimenting the queen on her devotion to the dying king. For at this point Eliza Acton (1799–1859) thought of herself as a poet of talent and had contributed verse to journals in Suffolk, where she had lived before moving to Bordyke House, in Tonbridge. But in Bordyke House it was the kitchen as well as the study that was to make her famous. In 1845 she published her *Modern Cookery*, which remained the most popular cookery book of its day, even for many years after Mrs Beeton published her own magnum opus. Miss Acton tested all but a handful of recipes on her own stove; and the few she didn't test she regarded as having come from unimpeachable sources. The mid-19th century saw the beginnings of the commercial food industry and Eliza Acton's book began to seem cumbersome and old-fashioned. She has become a popular adjunct to many well-run kitchens once more for three reasons: the growing popularity of cooking as a pastime as well as a necessity; the farsightedness of one or two publishing houses and the proselytising enthusiasm of some modern cookery writers and editors; and above all Eliza Acton's own literary ability allied with practicality.

vernacular with a lot of timber and composition-slate, with beautiful landscaping. But whereas Lyon's houses sold well in small groups in suburban London, here they were not popular enough to sell fast, and complications with two of the big financial backers left Span in severe difficulties. Ash itself has a lovely group of church, Charles II house, rectory and cricket pitch.

To the east, **Meopham** is a big village struggling along the road between Wrotham and Gravesend, but it is famous for its large, triangular village green with handsome windmill, cricket pitch and pavilion. The Cricketers' pub has a reputation for good food as well as beer. The downland between Ash and Meopham is an enchantment, with secluded villages and hamlets like **Ridley**, with a tiny turreted church, and **Stansted**: tip-tilted fields, barns, a pub, a pretty little flint church – all Perpendicular of around 1400 – and a little green in a hollow.

TONBRIDGE

The school that Sir Andrew Judd founded in 1553 is called Tonbridge School; the school that he didn't found is called Judd School. The first is north of the town, the second south; neither is much to look at, and between is the main street not much different from those of many towns of 30,000 souls except that, where the road crosses the Medway, high above stands a castle.

The prosperity of **Tonbridge** was assured when the Medway was made navigable as far as the town in the mid-18th century, but in the Middle Ages and earlier it was strategically important because it commanded the road to Hastings. Despite the bypass, the road through Tonbridge has never lost its importance, and if you don't have to drive through Tonbridge, it is best not to try. For though the town has spawned industry and sprawled at the edges,

the focus is still the High Street. You would be
hard put to describe the street as picturesque,
but north of the river there are some
individually interesting buildings including two
inns, the Rose and Crown and the Chequers,
and a double-gabled building next door to the
Chequers; off the High Street a road called
from time immemorial Bordyke ('the borough
ditch'), once part of the town's defence works,
later a street where among others lived Eliza
Acton, the Elizabeth David of the 19th century.
The old priory disappeared last century under
the railway goods yard. The local authority put
paid a few years ago to a row of half-timbered
houses in the High Street. But the parts of the
castle that Cromwell didn't knock about a bit
remain, domesticated with gardens and offices,
but impressive.

Castle, in fact, came before town. Tonbridge
probably derives from *dun-burh*, the castle on
the hill. The only hill is above Tonbridge, so
that leaves the castle mound, and for many
years Tonbridge was merely a cluster of
dwellings around the skirts of the castle. There
are signs of an Iron Age castle here; the Saxons
followed suit; the Normans constructed the
motte and bailey as they survive today: a huge
conical mound rising from a courtyard,
pleasantly grassed over. The Norman keep on
the motte was razed and what stands instead,
apart from lengths of curtain wall, is a massive
gatehouse from the reign of Edward I with
double drum towers and provision for two
portcullises. 'The gateway is perfect', wrote
Horace Walpole on passing this way in 1752,
'and the inclosure formed into a vineyard by a
Mr Hooker, to whom it belongs, and the walls
spread with fruit and the mount on which the
keep stood, planted in the same way.' The
vineyard is replaced by a park, otherwise the
description stands, with the addition of Mr
Hooker's charming Gothick range that now
serves as council offices.

Meopham

Royal Tunbridge Wells

Population: 58,141

Early Closing: Wed

Cashpoints: *Barclays* 84 Mount Pleasant Rd; *Lloyds* 82 Mount Pleasant Rd; *Midland* 86 High St, 105 Mount Pleasant Rd; *Nat West* 32 Mount Pleasant Rd, 89 Mount Pleasant Rd, 5 St John's Rd, Safeway – Vale Rd

Tourist Information: Civic Buildings

Attractions: Tunbridge Wells Museum and Art Gallery

Arts: The Assembly Halls, Trinity Arts Centre

Leisure: St John's Sports Centre

Cinema: Cannon 1, 2 and 3

By Road: London 38 miles (A26, A21, M25, A20), Maidstone 18 miles (A26)

By Rail: 50mins from London (London, Charing Cross to Hastings line). Direct services to Hastings and Sevenoaks. Connections to Ashford via Tonbridge

ROYAL TUNBRIDGE WELLS

The baptist chapel at **Tunbridge Wells** sits a stone's throw from the Church of King Charles the Martyr. Nobody today breaches the peace by stone-throwing, but it is more than likely that once they did. For the inhabitants of this inhospitable tract of Wealden forest were largely non-conformist of various persuasions, whereas the London court society visiting annually to take the waters and indulge themselves in pleasure were royalist and high church. The hills in this spot were Mount Ephraim, Mount Pleasant, Mount Sion; but the *haute monde* of the Restoration, who raised the money for their new church by subscription, insisted on dedicating it to King Charles I.

The Wells were discovered for society some years earlier by Lord North, returning to London from staying with Lord Abergavenny at Eridge and stumbling upon the chalybeate spring at the foot of a hill in a clearing that we now know as the Pantiles. The unpleasant ochre precipitation from the water on to the rock reminded him of medicinal waters he had seen in Germany. (There is a legend that the Devil had his nose singed in Sussex by St Dunstan, and dipped it in Tunbridge's water to cool it – hence the water's reddish tinge.) He took some to London, had its medicinal qualities confirmed, returned, became a new man, and was followed by Queen Henrietta Maria and her retinue, camping on the common and turning the English summer into a party.

The Wells never looked back. It was not grand, like Bath or Buxton, nor was it airy and spacious like Cheltenham, and for all its nearness it was not even easy to get to. The tracks of the Weald were notorious gluepots in bad weather: Horace Walpole grumbles about the difficulty of hiring a couple of horses hereabouts because the only accessible owner considered the roads too bad. But it had charm, lots of charm, and it had the health-giving waters to go with the more dubious pleasures of balls and gaming and theatre. (Kemble appeared here, in the theatre that has become more prosaically the Corn Exchange, and here Edmund Kean made his first appearance.)

Beau Nash stipulated that the waters should be taken between 7am and 9am leaving the rest of the day for the pleasures of society; a conscience-salving notion like drinking slimline tonic with a healthy slug of gin. The Pantiles, or the Walks, as it was then known, took shape very quickly. By 1637 it was a little street of shops and by 1687 it had been laid out with its characteristic and surviving arcade, which now comfortably incorporates buildings of only one vernacular but most periods, including everyone's favourite, a pretty little music gallery with a scrolly, curved ironwork balcony. The Pantiles is paved with flagstones, though the surface of bricks that gave it its name still exists at the end where the spring rises by the stuccoed Bath House with its imposing Tuscan pillars. The Pantiles is as remote from traffic as the streets of Venice, and though the Pantiles could hardly aspire to be, as Napoleon described the Piazza San Marco, the finest drawing room in Europe, it is the nearest thing an English summer will allow.

The grandest building in town is the King Charles church. Plain to the point of brick-box austerity outside, despite a gay little white cupola, within it is richly exotic: a royally decorative plaster ceiling by John Wetherel and Wren's plasterer Henry Doogood, moulded with a dozen deep wells ringed with fruit and flowers with cherub-countenanced winged putti in the interstices; the ceiling is supported on columns decorated with swags of fruit and flowers, commissioned from an Italian craftsman 200 years after the church was first consecrated but in character.

The Pantiles, Tunbridge Wells

Above a garden climbing Mount Pleasant, Decimus Burton laid out a crescent of houses in 1828, another row of houses that quickly became the Calverley Hotel, and a group of villas behind a big Doric arch. It may not be as sweeping a conception as the spa crescents of John Wood or John Carr, but it is fine, well-mannered, spacious but undemonstrative, and survives even the crass attack of a concrete multi-storey carpark placed adjacent in Crescent Road.

Trade flourished, the agony went out of puritanism (a grand Tuscan-porticoed Congregational church on Mount Pleasant has become a yuppie furnishing store), and the coming of the railway sealed the success of the town. The Victorians built big and bold, forgot the lesson of Burton, and Tunbridge Wells turned from a place for high society into a place for country people, a genteel place, a place to shop without being jostled, an easy place from which to travel to London or Glyndebourne.

Penshurst Place

West of Tonbridge on the B2027, **Leigh** has the look of an estate village, and indeed many of the cottages were built by Samuel Morley MP after his purchase of Hall Place in 1871. One of the largest village greens in Kent lies on the way to Hall Place, where the great attractions are the gardens and large lake with lakeside walks.

A gleam of water, a flag glimpsed over a low rise flying from a gatehouse, and there, beyond a big meadow, the wide sandstone north front of **Penshurst Place** is in view. It makes a brave sight, in a hollow but above the valley where the Eden joins the Medway. The house has been the home of the Sidney family since 1552. The present owner is William Philip Sidney, Viscount de L'Isle, VC, and a descendant of another gentleman and warrior, Philip Sidney, born at Penshurst Place in 1559, best remembered for the lambent lines:

*With how sad steps, O Moon, thou climb'st the
skies!*
How silently, and with how wan a face!

among a famous body of verse. The house goes
back much further than the Sidneys'
occupation. There was a house here at the
Norman Conquest, but the heart of the present
great house was built by Sir John de Pulteney
in 1340.

The visitor approaches from the south
through herbaceous borders and yew hedges: a
formal garden of great splendour within a
mellow brick wall, but almost touchingly
English with its rows of old-fashioned, full-
sized, Cox's orange pippin trees flanking the
path leading to the house. 'Then hath thy
orchard fruit, thy garden flowers,/Fresh as the
ayre, and new as are the houres,' Ben Jonson
wrote of Penshurst, for our time as well as his.

The garden gives access through a free-
standing tower, once part of a system of
fortifications, to the great 14th-century hall
built by Sir John de Pulteney, merchant prince
and four times Lord Mayor of London. Three
and a half centuries later Celia Fiennes
travelled by Penshurst and made her famous
judgment: 'The house is but old, large roomes
and stone staires and windows, a good hall
and gallery full of good old pictures, and other
roomes of State, no furniture but old tapistry
hangings . . .' which, still, is not far off the
mark. The hall is complete and unspoilt, down
to the central hearth where an open fire burned
(the only alteration in the six centuries since Sir
John first feasted here is that the hole in the
roof for the smoke to escape has been blocked).
The hall is massive for the time:

62ft long, 39ft wide, and 60ft high. The great
chestnut roof of crown posts rest on walls
braced with life-sized figures of glum peasants
beneath, a standing reproach to the feasting
below, though old Ben Jonson again,

Sir Philip Sidney
Sir Philip Sidney was the
very archetype of the
Renaissance gentleman: a
scholar, poet and warrior,
chivalrous in love and war,
languidly reclining under a
tree in the portrait by the
fashionable (and great)
miniaturist Isaac Oliver;
'curteous, valiant, and
liberall,' as Edmund Spenser
mourned him on his death,
'godlike' in the florid
tribute by Ben Jonson, he
was famed throughout
Europe for his charm and
qualities. He was born at
Penshurst Place in 1554.
One godfather was John
Russell, 1st Earl of Bedford.
The other was Queen
Mary's husband, Philip II,
King of Spain, after whom
Philip Sidney was named.
The Christian name
survives in the family to
this day, but the
Catholicism died with
Philip, who vehemently
espoused the Protestant
cause all his days and died
fighting for it. He wrote his
enduring prose work,
Arcadia, after retiring to the
country because he had
opposed Queen Elizabeth's
planned marriage to the
Catholic Duke of Anjou and
had aroused her ire. He
started his poetry cycle
Astrophel and Stella,
comprising 108 sonnets and
11 songs, in 1575 when he
fell in love with Penelope
Devereux. He stopped in
1583 when he married
Frances Walsingham.
Mortally wounded in an
attack on a Spanish
garrison in the Low
Countries, he wrote a poem,
'The Wounded Thigh', and
had it set to music and
sung to him. He was buried
in St Paul's Cathedral.

celebrating his visit to Penshurst, wrote:

And though thy walls be of the countrey stone,
They are rear'd with no mans ruine, no mans
grone,
There's none, that dwell about them, wish them
down;
But all come in, the farmer and the clowne.

Off the hall, steps lead to the small but fine gothic undercroft of a solar above; the solar itself is now the state dining room, still used by the family for special occasions. The huge oak table is laid with a Rockingham dinner service made for William IV, whose illegitimate daughter married Lord de L'Isle. At least three paintings of Sir Philip Sidney preside among the other family groups and portraits. Most of the rest of the house is new, if only by the standard of Pulteney's. It was built in the 15th and 16th centuries (and the handsome north front largely rebuilt in the 19th after years of neglect). The so-called Buckingham wing was more likely built by the Duke of Bedford, brother of Henry V. It leads to the Long Gallery, designed in the fashion set by Cranmer at Hampton Court, full of family portraits, and with handsomely pilastered Jacobean panelling.

West of the house is Penshurst church, remarkable mainly for the Sidney family chapel, rebuilt in 1820, but around the tomb of Sir Stephen de Penchester, who died in 1299 and who owned the previous Penshurst Place (known, like the village, as Penchester). The remains of the Sidneys down the ages are here but not the family's presiding genius: Sir Philip Sidney was mortally wounded fighting the Spaniards in the Low Countries in 1586 and was buried in St Paul's Cathedral. His tomb was lost with the cathedral in the Great Fire of London.

The village is delightful. There is a good 18th-century-fronted rectory to the west of the church with handsome doorcase and eaves; the rest of the village is mostly a mixture of real and nicely-judged pastiche Tudor, with a sense of the countryside invading all round.

Chiddingstone is nothing much; but the nothing much is near-perfect: a short row of handsome Tudor houses preserved in its entirety by the National Trust, a church, and Chiddingstone Castle set in a lovely park. The church is 14th century, spaciously rebuilt in the 17th after a fire. It has a fine Perpendicular tower, a good 17th-century font with Jacobean font cover, a mausoleum in the churchyard for the lords of the manor, the Streatfeilds, one of whom is buried under an iron slab within the nave inscribed: 'Loe here the copes of Richard Streatfeilde greene in yeres but ripe in faith'. The Streatfeilds lived in the castle, originally simply High Street House, but crenellated in the 19th century. Due north is Bough Beech Reservoir, managed as a nature reserve. It is a popular place for watching birds, which can be seen from the road south of Winkhurst Green, although there is no public access to the water.

Hever Castle

As manor houses go, **Hever** is big. As castles go, it is, in the old *Private Eye* catchphrase, tiny but perfectly formed. In Tudor times it belonged to the Boleyns. Notoriously, Henry VIII came to stay, and carried away a wife. But at the height of their pomp, the Boleyns could never have dreamt of Hever as grand as it became when an American millionaire called William Waldorf Astor bought it in 1903. He might have done the normal thing: taken it down stone by stone and re-erected it in the USA. Instead, he did the next best thing: left it where it was, rescued it from the farmyard decrepitude into which it had fallen, built a Tudor hamlet in the grounds to accommodate his weekend guests (instead of spoiling the castle by extending it), diverted the River Eden to create a 40-acre lake, before the lake built a grand stone terrace and

Iron

The Garden of England was the Black Country of England during the Middle Ages. Villages rang to the sound of forge hammers and the protests of farmers and cloth manufacturers. The cannons as well as the ships of the king's navy came from the Kent and Sussex forests. The British were working the iron ore of the Weald before the arrival of the Romans; the Romans carried on the industry and so did the Saxons, but in their case mostly in the Forest of Dean in Gloucestershire. Proximity to London told, and by the Middle Ages and particularly during the reign of Henry VIII a belt of Kentish Wealden villages from Biddenden to Cowden were making iron: Lamberhurst (where the railings were made for St Paul's Cathedral), Goudhurst, Horsmonden, Ashurst, Tonbridge (with another iron foundry near Bayham Abbey), Hawkhurst and Cranbrook. Products included nails, arrow heads, bands to line cartwheels, and firebacks.

The sites of the industry can still be found through local names: commonly Furnace Pond and Hammer Pond (created by clay dams to operate furnaces bellows or power hammers), Furnace Farm, Hammer Dyke, Hammer Stream and Forge Farm. The industry was already declining (for lack of fuel among other things) when Abraham Darby of Staffordshire discovered how to employ cheap coke in smelting iron.

crescent-shaped colonnaded loggia, and between loggia and house laid out a formal Italian garden filled with antique sculpture from the Roman and Venetian empires, porphyry columns from Rome, huge oil jars from Pompeii, gods and godesses, naked athletes, Ganymede and his eagle, sarcophagi, a sepulchral chest and a cinerary chest, Byzantine lions and enough fountain basins alone to have denuded Rome. There is a rustic loggia to one side of the garden and beside that a garden on a hillside tinkling with small streams and waterfalls.

In short, it is not very English, but it is very wonderful. From without, the castle itself is perfect, and perfectly genuine. Inside it is a gloriously extravagant, self-indulgent fake, from the portraits hopefully labelled 'attributed to Holbein' to the sumptuously carved wainscotting. The carving, like a lot of the furnishing, is richly Edwardian imitation Tudor; so in that sense it is the real thing: no more true Tudor than Charles Laughton's Henry VIII, but a masterpiece in its own right, larger than life.

Lord Astor, as he was to become, had bought a house dating from the early 13th century, built by one William de Hever. In 1384, licence to crenellate was obtained by Sir John de Cobham, the same Sir John who fortified Cooling Castle, and he left the castle in much the same basic shape as it is today, with entrance gained by a wooden drawbridge over a moat and through a massive crenellated and machicolated gatehouse that dominates the building; it is so big in proportion that it forms the whole of one side of the courtyard within. The door to the screens passage opposite the gatehouse is original; and so is the wooden panelling in the long gallery above. There are relics of Anne Boleyn and pieces of historical interest; the rest is fantasy incorporating little period found objects as modern artists have come to call them; but houses are for living in and all old houses that aren't ruins change with the generations; all one can ask is that the changes are sympathetic. William Wardorf Astor's are sympathetic, imaginative, luxurious, wholly delightful and deserve their continuing popularity.

Edenbridge has large GLC overspill estates and growing light industry. Its axis is the long main street crossing the river halfway down. At this point the best of the town survives: a big timber-framed 15th-century house built for Sir William Taylour, Lord Mayor of London, the Crown Hotel, which is a former coaching inn, with its sign overhanging the street, tanneries and a watermill in use until 1968 and now a restaurant.

The plain inscriptions on the graves in **Cowden** churchyard record the deaths on 19 November 1726 of Richard Still, aged 66, and on 6 June 1730 of his wife Mary, aged 72. Nothing remarkable there, except that the memorial slabs are rusty. Cowden is deep in the High Weald, just inside the Sussex border, and here until northern coal took over from the diminishing forests of Kent, iron was a cottage industry. Richard Still was an ironmaster, one of the many whose families lie beneath iron slabs in Wealden villages, where the only other evidence of the industry that died with its masters is a place name. At Cowden it is Furnace Farm and Furnace Pond.

Untouched, almost, by time and tourism, Cowden is basically a street of weatherboarded and tile-hung cottages starting with the Crown Inn and ending not much more than a 100yds west. The church is 14th century with a later north aisle, spectacular timbers supporting the tower, and a fine series of crown posts in nave and chancel. Outside, the tower turns into a splay-footed spire and is prettily shingled from the eaves of the roof upwards. Close to the village is **Waystrode Manor**, a 14th–15th-century house (not open) surrounded by a lovely, informal 6½-acre garden full of carefully labelled plants – a great plus for enthusiasts on opening days.

For miles around the 170ft high Gothick tower of **Hadlow**, 'May's Folly', is a landmark. The tower of William Beckford's notorious Fonthill had already collapsed a decade before Walter Barton May embarked on his own homage to Beckford in 1838. Hadlow Castle, he called his building. Most of the rest of the building has been demolished now, but the gatehouse on the village street near the church still stands, and May employed a navy architect to ensure the stability of his amazing four-storeyed octagonal brick tower crowned with pinnacles. May's estranged wife lived at Fish Hall nearby; she was Walter Pater's godmother, and Pater spent many of his childhood days in Hadlow. Later, Pater fictionalised Walter May in one of his *Imaginary Portraits* as the eccentric Sebastian van Storck, dying alone in an upper room of an old tower.

St Mary's is a pleasant little church, basically Early English, but it is most remarkable for the so called Coverdale Chair within, a 19th-century concoction from a range of ornate 16th- and 17th-century carvings.

A driver motoring too fast through **Tudeley** will miss the church. It is a tiny building almost sitting in a barnyard, with a little 18th-century brick tower capped by a short, shingled spire. It is also the finest expression in England of modern religious art: better in its totality than the well-intentioned jumble of Coventry Cathedral; better in detail than anything in Canterbury, say, or Chichester. Chichester has a stained glass window by Marc Chagall. Tudeley has 12.

To recapitulate: Chagall was a Russian who in his early years painted pictures of peasant life as intense as icons; in his first years in Paris the turmoil of early-20th-century art crossed

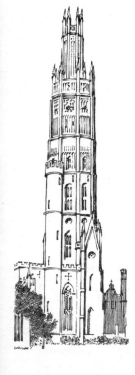

Hadlow Castle

with his visionary qualities and is sometimes
said to have slightly sentimentalised his
painting; but his discovery of the techniques of
stained glass in his old age led to a great
flowering of his art. Sir Henry and Lady
d'Avigdor Goldsmid, of the big Jacobean house
in the parish, Somerhill, commissioned an east
window from Chagall in 1963 to commemorate
their daughter, Sarah, who had died that year
in a sailing accident.

Chagall confronted the subject directly: in a
window dominated by Christ on the cross
beneath a great red nimbus-like rainbow and
surrounded by angels and mourning women,
the subject is treated hieratically but tenderly: a
young woman drifts in the waves, like Ophelia
in Millais's famous painting but not stiff in a
studio stream; embraced instead in an element
merging with the blue of heaven. Higher up
she is seen climbing a ladder towards heaven
and riding a red horse symbolising happiness.
Following the initial commission for the east
window alone, the project grew and the last of
the 12 windows was installed in 1985. The
effect on entering through the south door is
extraordinary. The windows are
overwhelmingly blue, and the submarine effect
is enhanced by the green marbled barrel-
vaulted nave ceiling of about 1765. But as the
sun moves round it shines through yellow
windows in the south aisle. All five chancel
windows are blue, but one little quatrefoil light
contains a yellow head like the sun itself. The
mists of colour half reveal fleeting angels,
animals peering through long tendrils of
vegetation; a tender evocation of the mystery
of Christian salvation by a wandering Russian
Jew.

4 Maidstone, Mid Kent and the Weald

High up at Castle Hill on a country road between Horsmonden and Brenchley there is a sudden clear panorama to the north across the Medway Valley, over the greensand hills, to the North Downs. In the intervening countryside are woods, hop gardens, orchards and fields, with the crisp white cowls of hop kilns. This High Weald is a countryside so green and golden, with such a plenitude of timber, with such ample hills and gently folded valleys that it, above all others in Kent, has led to that shop-worn phrase, 'the Garden of England'; a cliché that says nothing about the toil of centuries that made this place rich.

For this was once the Andredsweald, a primeval forest where a few intrepid woodcutters and charcoal burners eked a living until the Middle Ages, when oak began to be felled for shipbuilding and to feed the furnaces of the iron industry. All the placenames ending in '-ley' and '-den' and '-hurst' date from the medieval Wealden clearances. And now although this great swathe of beautiful countryside still looks densely wooded seen from the greensand ridge anywhere between

Oast houses

Westerham and Wye, it contains some of the richest agricultural land in the county.

Above the Weald sit Sevenoaks, West Malling, Maidstone, Boughton Monchelsea; and some of the country beyond is so remote, so lost in heavy woodland that a few years ago a car that went off the Gravesend road where it begins to descend sharply to Wrotham simply went missing for a few days. Further across, in the mysterious woodland behind Holly Hill, is **Luddesdown**, a tiny hamlet with a church and a house, Luddesdown Court, that dates back to the 11th or 12th century. A little further south is **Dode**, which has only one building, about the size of a decent garden shed, but which was the Norman church of a village that disappeared with the Black Death in the 14th century. From Dode the track emerges at **Birling**, where there is still a working smithy, and on to **Snodland**, an ancient crossing point on the Medway for the Pilgrims' Way. This is dominated now by the massive papermill, just as Cuxton and Halling are dominated by the cement factories as the river sweeps around to the north through the wide, beautiful gap in the North Downs bridged by the spectacular viaduct of the M2.

MAIDSTONE

When Kent stretched from Greenwich to Dover, Penenden Heath was, as nearly as mattered, dead centre. If there were any important disputes to be settled, it was to Penenden that the litigants came. Today Penenden is a stretch of green surviving in a northern suburb of Maidstone. Even at Domesday, Maidstone was quite big. There were six mills, a church, four and a half fisheries yielding 450 eels in tax, and two salt houses. But whatever primacy the town had in the Middle Ages, it forfeited by being heavily involved in the 1554 rebellion against Queen Mary: the queen stripped the town of its

'Mad' John Ball
'Mad' John Ball held some opinions that seem odd to us: he believed for instance that bastards could not succeed to the kingdom of heaven. If he was mad, though, it was 'nor' nor' west' only, in Hamlet's phrase. He was a priest who preached on the popular texts, 'When Adam dalf, and Eve span,/Who was thanne a gentilman?', which was highly seditious in 1381, when popular anger ran high.

Ball was, in fact, a dangerously popular demagogue, and as such was several times restrained in the cells beneath the Archbishop of Canterbury's palace at Maidstone. He was also defrocked and excommunicated. None of this stopped John Ball from preaching to the disaffected. He had lost his pulpit, so he preached in churchyards and marketplaces. When Wat Tyler raised a rebellion in 1381, one of his first objectives was to release Ball from his prison cell. Ball accompanied Wat Tyler in the heady ride to Blackheath, and then rode to the Tower of London, and at last to the interview with the king at Smithfield where Tyler was treacherously cut down. Ball fled, but was captured and brought before the king at St Albans. He was sentenced to be hanged, drawn, and quartered, and the king personally watched the execution on 15 July 1381.

Maidstone

Population: 87,068

Early Closing: Wed

Market Day: Tue

Cashpoints: *Barclays* 17 Middle Row; *Lloyds* 18 Week St; *Midland* 16 High St; *Nat West* 3 High St, 91 High St, 197 Sutton Rd Shepway

Tourist Information: The Gatehouse, Old Palace Gardens

Attractions: Allington Castle, Leeds Castle, Museum and Art Gallery, Stoneacre* (3m SE), Tyrwhitt-Drake Museum of Carriages*

Arts: Hazlitt Theatre

Leisure: Mote Swimming Baths, Westborough Sports Centre, YMCA Sports Centre

By Road: London 37 miles (M20, A20), Ashford 19 miles (A20), Tunbridge Wells 18 miles (A26)

By Rail: 1hr from London (London, Victoria to Ashford line). Direct services from Maidstone East station to Ashford and Sevenoaks via Otford; direct services from Maidstone West station to Chatham and Rochester via Strood

charter of incorporation. Her successor, however, 'of hir great clemencie', as William Lambarde put it, writing not long after the event, 'hath not onely restored the place to a new incorporation, but endowed it also with greater Privilege, apparelling the Mayor with the authoritie of a Justice of the Peace . . . and creating the towne it selfe a Borough, enabled to have voice in Parleament'.

The county town has never looked back. Defoe found it a town 'of very great business and Trade, and yet full of Gentry, of Mirth, and of good Company'. Today, for all the damage done by war and 'business and trade', there is always something to catch the eye. There is an overhanging Jacobean shop front in Bank Street with florid coloured pargeting modelling the Prince of Wales's feathers, and the royal arms of 1607 either side of a window with an arch supported by mullions and splendid caryatids. The old-fashioned fish shop of John Bradford and Sons, in Earl Street, with its open front and marble slabs sloping towards the street, sports a life-size fisherman above the shop in a yellow oilskin, grinning widely and proffering a large salmon. In Bank Street, there are crossed sporting rifles, and on Gabriel's Hill a great golden boot is suspended outside a shoe shop founded in the 18th century.

Among all this, the High Street at its widest point splits into two (one branch becomes Bank Street) and flows like a river around the late-18th-century Town Hall. Built of red brick and Portland Stone, rococo plasterwork and painted decoration within, it can be seen by appointment. The Town Hall displays its clock with a dash, like the White Rabbit with his big fob watch. In Earl Street is the high, wide and handsome house built for Andrew Broughton, Mayor of Maidstone, and the man who pronounced the sentence of death upon King Charles I. In St Faith Street is the Elizabethan, brick-built Chillington Manor, now the museum.

General Fairfax led his Parliamentary troops up Gabriel's Hill to defeat the Royalists in one of the key Civil War battles in Kent. At the top of the hill a plaque marks the building that was the Bell Inn when Pepys visited, and enjoyed, Maidstone in 1669: 'I did buy and send to our Inne, the Bell, a dish of fresh fish; and so having walked all round the town, and find it very pretty as most towns I ever saw, though not very big, and people of good fashion in it, we to our Inne to dinner, and had a good dinner, and after dinner a barber came to me and there trimmed me . . .' On the banks of the Medway is a lovely group of buildings: the Archbishop's Palace, the medieval priests' college and the parish church of All Saints.

The palace was built by Archbishop Islip early in the 14th century, but the façade is Elizabethan. The undercroft is still medieval, and it was probably from a cell here that 'Mad' John Ball, the excommunicated priest who incited Wat Tyler to rebellion, was triumphantly released by the revolutionaries. Over the road are the palace stables, basically ragstone, but with a projecting timber-framed porch with herring-bone brick work between the timbers. The stable block is now the Tyrwhitt-Drake Museum, sheltering a beautifully maintained collection of carriages and coaches.

The college and church were both founded by Archbishop Courtenay in 1395–7. The most impressive remaining part of the college is the battlemented gatehouse, built in three storeys. One room fills the whole top floor, and there is a big vaulted entrance for carriages and a smaller one for pedestrians. Part of the college is now the Kent Music School, and part the sea cadets' headquarters. The parish church is on the grand scale too. Pepys climbed the 78ft tower 'and had a noble view'. There is still a complete set of chancel stalls (with misericords

William Grocyn
A tablet on the facade of Kent Music School in Maidstone commemorates an obscure medieval divine called William Grocyn. Why? Grocyn wrote little, and little of what he wrote has survived. He was not a native of Maidstone and may even have gone to live there only because he needed the money that went with the position of master of the priest's college (the Kent Music School is in what was the master's house). But Grocyn was eminent in his day, a great Greek scholar who taught Thomas More, a generous man who lent money to Erasmus to the detriment of his own welfare, and whom, not surprisingly in the circumstances, Erasmus described as 'the most upright and best of all Britons'. More than this his goodness held his friends in thrall: he was a great talker and a great wit, and Thomas More, writing to another scholar in their circle in 1504, said, 'Grocyn is in your absence the master of my life'. As a conservative churchman, he might have become famous historically in the troubles that surrounded the schism with Rome, but he died aged about 73 in 1519. He was a native of Wiltshire, educated at Winchester and New College, Oxford, where he became a fellow and made his name as a scholar before moving on to a number of small church preferments and finally to Maidstone, where he died and was buried in the churchyard of All Saints.

The Wyatts

The Wyatts of Allington Castle were a tempestuous family in tempestuous times. Sir Henry Wyatt opposed Richard III's annointment as king in 1483, and was imprisoned for the two years of the reign. Henry VII succeeded Richard and Sir Henry became a privy counsellor. In 1492 he bought Allington Castle, where he lived until his death in 1537.

His illustrious son Thomas, poet, courtier and diplomat, was born in about 1503. His father was a friend of another Kentish grandee, Sir Thomas Boleyn. In May 1536, when Anne Boleyn's alleged infidelities brought her to the scaffold, Thomas Wyatt was briefly imprisoned in the Tower. ('In May my wealth and eke my life, I say/Have stood so oft in such perplexity,' he wrote in a sonnet.) He was on the king's business in the West Country in 1542 when he died of a fever. His poetry – educated and energetic, and the first adaptation of the Italian verse form, the sonnet, into English – was published after his death.

His only son Thomas – pugnacious, cheerful, and apparently without his father's intellectual qualities – served the crown faithfully until Queen Mary announced her intention of marrying Philip of Spain; this Thomas regarded as a dishonour to the realm. He led 4000 men in rebellion to London, but was betrayed, captured and beheaded.

including a grinning cook brandishing a ladle), and at the one end of the church, on the west wall, is an extraordinary monument to the Astleys of the manor house (formerly the Archbishop's Palace): four full-length, elongated standing figures, wrapped in shrouds. The chancel north aisle was once the chantry for the Corpus Christi fraternity, whose hall, now part of Whitbread-Fremlin's brewery, is at the river end of Earl Street.

The most famous Maidstone view, however, is from the opposite bank of the Medway, below the market and the law courts. The church and college sit high above the river, and there is a lovely tree-lined walk below them to a small park a couple of hundred yards upriver. As you leave Maidstone on the A20 going north-west, a road leads off to the right, past Allington shopping centre and on for a mile until it turns into a country lane and peters out at a vegetable garden by the Medway. The garden is run by the Carmelite friars of **Allington Castle**. The castle's battlements were built by Simon de Penchester in 1281, and by the 16th century the Wyatt family lived there. Sir Henry Wyatt built the range of buildings across the middle of the courtyard, of which the long gallery, a new and fashionable concept imported from Italy, is the jewel. His son, Sir Thomas Wyatt, in turn imported the sonnet form from Italy into English literature. He was a courtier high in the esteem of Henry VIII but he seems not to have wholeheartedly reciprocated Henry's pleasure in his company. In an 'epistolary satire', he explains why he prefers home rather than to live 'under the awe of lordly looks'.

I cannot speak and look like a saint.
Use wiles for wit and make deceit a pleasure
And call craft council, for profit still to paint
I cannot wrest the law to fill the coffer,

With innocent blood to fed myself fat,
And do most hurt where most help I offer.

And indeed Holbein's chalk portrait of
Wyatt (at Windsor Castle) shows a man with
an uncompromising gaze. His son seems to
have been the same: he led a rebellion against
Queen Mary's marriage to Philip of Spain, and
died under the axe on Tower Hill. By 1905 the
castle was a ruin, but Sir Martin Conway
lovingly restored and rebuilt it. It is now a
Carmelite retreat, but much of the architectural
history of its first four centuries remains visible
and it is well worth visiting.

A significant part of English history began
at **Aylesford**, which straddles the Medway to
the west. A lovely medieval bridge, the first of
many on the Medway, leads straight into the
jumbled old heart of the village. This is the first
easily fordable spot on the river and is where
the brothers Hengist and Horsa (who may not
have existed) led the Jutes (who were real
enough) against Vortigern and the native
British. The Jutes won, and their settlement of
Kent established the beginnings of modern
England.

Aylesford's High Street is dominated by the
church and leads to the lovely Friars, built in
the Middle Ages for Carmelite monks. It was
closed at the Reformation, and re-established
later. The Carmelites returned in 1949. There is
a Bailey bridge to relieve pressure on the old
bridge, because Aylesford has become home to
huge papermills and associated, voraciously
spreading warehouses.

Around about, the countryside is littered
with the remains of prehistoric burial places,
principally the fallen megaliths of the *Countless
Stones* (or *Little Kit's Coty*) just below the
Pilgrims' Way, and *Kit's Coty House* just above:
'three stones staying upright and a great round
one lying on them of great bigness, although
not so big as those on Salisbury-

Neolithic Kent
Some five thousand years ago Neolithic man left the first tangible monuments of human life in Kent. Kit's Coty, the intriguingly named Countless Stones (intriguing because there are only a few of them), the Addington Stones, and the Coldrum at Trottiscliffe are the remains of long barrows, or burial places, built of local sarsen stones. Archaeological evidence suggests that they were built by people who emigrated up the Iberian coastline and along France before settling along the Medway Valley. Apart from the upper Medway, there have been finds of flint implements and pottery in other riverside locations along the Dour Valley (which emerges at Dover), the Stour, the Darent and the Cray. These folk were clearly great travellers: many of the finds include implements from widely flung areas: an axe-hammer from Cornwall, an adze from the Lake District. The best collection of these Kentish archaeological finds is in Maidstone Museum.

Hops

plain, but certainly it is a thing of great antiquity, and I mightily glad to see it', wrote Pepys. All that has happened since Pepys saw it is that the Neolithic burial chamber has been ringed by very necessary iron railings. There are stirring views across the Medway Valley.

Boxley had Kent's only Cistercian Abbey, founded in 1146. It became notorious for the hoax its monks perpetrated on superstitious pilgrims by manipulating the 'miraculous' movements of the Rood of Grace with wires. The abbey was razed in 1538 but the superb 186ft long ragstone tithe barn survives. The village is beautiful, with a long green leading to the church, and the soft downland above running from here to Ashford. The downland is ragged at the fringes where the hurricane of 1987 did its worst, but in Boxley Warren, just above the Pilgrims' Way, the yew and a few box trees have survived.

East of Maidstone is **Bearsted** where Wat Tyler gathered his followers in 1381 before marching on the Archbishop's Palace at Maidstone. Some centuries later, and in slightly less violent circumstances, Alfred Mynn, the first fast round-arm bowler, used the slope of Bearsted green cricket pitch to aid his run up. In 1903 the poet Edward Thomas lived for almost a year in Ivy Cottage, a 'pretty old house on the village green'. A little south of Bearsted, at **Otham** – but devilishly difficult to find – is Stoneacre, one of the most beautiful yeoman's houses remaining in England. In truth it is more a re-creation than an original, but the restoration work carried out in the 1920s was to a very high standard. Enjoyment begins at the delightful visitor's door, on the east front, promising high quality beyond. That promise is instantly redeemed by the Great Hall with its original oak screens. The magnificent kingpost, formed from a cluster of columns, is both rare and aesthetically pleasing

– remarks which are applicable to the whole house. Surrounding it is a garden of great charm, its tendency to darkness offset by simple touches like the addition of a white garden based on that at *Sissinghurst Castle*.

When **Leeds Castle** was first opened to the public in 1976 there was a notice beside the drive through the park, 'Golf balls have priority'. Today visitors are not so intimidated, and are encouraged to take the long and lovely walk through the informal grounds to which were added, in 1988, a remarkably elaborate grotto and maze. The castle itself stands on two islands in the great moat – more a lake – formed by damming the little river Len. The castle certainly existed in the 12th century, maybe earlier; but Edward I took it over in 1272, the first year of his reign, and gave it to Eleanor, his queen. For the next two centuries it remained part of the Queen of England's dower. Edward I built the gloriette (the building linked to the main castle by a bridge), and Henry VIII added its top floor. The visitors' entrance to the castle is through a Norman barrel-vaulted undercroft opposite the gloriette. Much of the main castle was built in the 19th century, and much has been adapted to 20th-century comforts since, including good facilities for disabled visitors. So in a sense, not much of it is any more authentic than the inside of *Hever*, but seen from the park it is romantically beautiful. The rooms have been made into splendid showpieces: there are Brussels tapestries, a Flemish triptych, and a 16th-century Gothic staircase with a fine carved figure of a crusader and dog at the top of the banister. One corridor is full of watercolours by the pre-impressionist, Constantin Guys, and the seminar room displays a late Monet canvas of the Salute seen from the other side of the Grand Canal, a grand Degas pastel of a dancer resting, two Pissarros (one a snowscape painted in the year of the first

Hops

Hops are as British as roast beef and bingo; or so it now seems. Pliny records them in the first century AD, and the Romans grew them as an asparagus-like vegetable. They have remained a wild plant in Kentish hedgerows. Cultivated hop gardens first became part of the Kentish agricultural industry during the reign of Edward III (1327–77), imported by Flemish immigrants. Even then, there was opposition from the vested interest of herbalists: English ale was flavoured with cloves and cinnamon, and in 1426 a Maidstone man was accused of 'putting into beer an unwholesome weed called a hoppe'. Henry VIII, too, was urged to ban hops. By then the battle was won and lost; in the mid-15th century an English dictionary, *Promptorium Parvulorium*, defined a 'hoppe' as a 'sede for beyre'.

Oast houses, where the hops were dried in the heat from a furnace beneath a slatted floor, are an invention of the last two centuries (the square kilns, by and large, 18th century, the round kilns 19th century). However, the EEC subsidy for hop growing is tiny, so as dwarf hops replace tall bines, and acreage shrinks under pressure of changing drinking fashions (lager needs fewer hops), the future of oast houses as an integral part of the landscape seems to rest on their conversion to quaint homes for commuters.

impressionist exhibition), a delicious Renoir landscape with the Sacre Coeur under construction in the background, a Fantin Latour flowerpiece, a Toulouse Lautrec, a Boudin beach scene and seascape, and a lovely little Vuillard of peaches and a flask of wine. It was in this room that an Israeli-Egyptian settlement was reached, before the Camp David talks.

Further east **Lenham** is set in rich farming land and built round two adjoining squares, with the church behind a medieval lychgate in the south-west corner, a big aisled barn just beyond that, and a variety of tile-hung and fine timber-framed houses around the square. A few yards away in the Faversham Road, one small building with great blocks of stones for the arch of its doorway stands out because it is built of ragstone. This was the Lenham lockup.

On the road towards Headcorn is an exceptional black-and-white timber-framed house with figures carved in the brackets of the overhang. The church is of mixed periods but has windows in the nave with that loveliest of all Decorated patterning, reticulated tracery. There is a fine Jacobean pulpit.

South through narrow lanes, and high on the ridge is **Boughton Malherbe**. The manor house beside the lovely church was home to the Wotton family for centuries. In his biography of Sir Henry Wotton, Izaak Walton referred to Boughton having 'the advantage of a large Prospect' and he did not overstate the case. It is still possible to leave the traffic of the Weald on summer days and drive up here to solitude and the chance to study an immense panorama stretching beyond Tenterden to Rye and the sea.

Still on the greensand ridge, but west a few miles **Boughton Monchelsea Place** lies in close embrace with Boughton Monchelsea church. The church, behind a lovely medieval lychgate, has been spoilt by restoration but there are

Lenham

wonderful views from the churchyard of the manor house's deerpark below and for 14 miles over the Weald beyond. The herd of fallow deer in the park has been there since at least 1669. The house is basically Elizabethan, and took on something approaching its appearance today in 1575. There is an unpretentious little walled garden.

Close to the village is **Linton Park**, which can be seen for miles on the approach from the other direction, through the Weald. Its white stucco front has a big Corinthian portico and is on the very edge of the greensand ridge, so that the north front is two storeys high, but the south is three. Walpole visited Linton in 1757, and wrote 'the house is fine, and stands like the citadel of Kent; the whole county is its garden'. Today the house is not open, but a public footpath runs through the beautiful park close to the north front.

Sutton Valence, perched, French style, on the greensand ridge overlooking the Low Weald has a public school and some fine private dwellings in the local ragstone. The ruins of the 12th-century Sutton Valence Castle stand in the grounds of the Old Parsonage.

Turning back towards Maidstone it is easy to miss the **Loose Valley** which lies under the A229. The valley has a fascinating history, reflected in the houses which line it. It has known great wealth and poverty – now it is again much sought after. Loose was a wool village and it still has the 15th-century half-timbered Wool House, probably once a fulling mill. Owned by the National Trust it is open on written application. A little higher upstream is the Old Mill House, its mill race converted to a waterfall. Lower down is the historic Hayle Paper Mill which has produced high quality hand-made paper for centuries. Only an industrial archaeologist could find it pretty but the refurbished Hayle Mill cottages (upstream) certainly are, as is Upper Crisbrook Mill with

Country Houses
The 17th and 18th centuries
transformed the face of
England. The Renaissance
arrived late but when it
came it took a specifically
English form. Concluding
the first volume of his great
History of England with a
survey of the state of the
nation in 1685, Macaulay
wrote: 'There is perhaps no
class of dwellings so
pleasing as the rural seats
of the English gentry. In
the parks and pleasure
grounds, nature, dressed
yet not disguised by art,
wears her most alluring
form. In the buildings,
good sense and good taste
combine to produce a
happy union of the
comfortable and the
graceful.' Nothing could
better sum up the English
inheritance, and nowhere is
it better seen than in Kent.
By repute, Inigo Jones built
Chevening, and the
proportions of this
singularly beautiful house
suggest that he did at least
have a hand in it.
Cobham's central range,
Bridge House, Brabourne,
Bourne Park, Godinton
Park, Wateringbury Place,
Matfield, Finchcocks,
Mereworth's villa translated
from the Veneto: the
builders of these houses
were not especially rich or
cultured, but their houses
possess an irreplacable
singularity, beauty and
historical significance.

an interesting memorial in its charming garden
to two scout leaders killed during World War I.
None of these buildings is open but they can
all be studied from the narrow road which
leads down to **Tovil**, an unlovely suburb of
Maidstone.

It is only a short journey from here to **East
Farleigh**, which, with its 14th-century five-
arched tunnel-vaulted bridge, is in hop country
and is the start, just beyond the spreading
southern outskirts of Maidstone, of a beautiful
stretch of the river Medway, where even the
choleric William Cobbett felt constrained to
write, in one of his *Rural Rides*:

*From Maidstone to this place (Merryworth) is about
seven miles, and these are the finest seven miles that
I have ever seen in England or any where else. The
Medway is to your left, with its meadows about a
mile wide . . . From Maidstone to Merryworth, I
should think that there were hop-gardens on one
half of the way on both sides of the road. Then
looking across the Medway, you see hop-gardens
and orchards two miles deep, on the side of a gently
rising ground: and this continues with you all the
way from Maidstone to Merryworth. The orchards
form a great feature of the country; and the
plantations of Ashes and of Chestnuts that I
mentioned before, add greatly to the beauty.*

The quotation is worth having at length
because the scene is virtually unchanged.

West Farleigh, a mile or so west, is not
much more than a hamlet with a church. The
latter has an 18th-century family pew for the
owners of West Farleigh Hall, one of the
Georgian brick houses with which the
neighbourhood abounds. There is a walled
garden (open once a year) at the Hall for which
bird's-eye drawings by Thomas Badeslade still
exist. The sketches show that little has been
changed in the garden since the publication of
the drawings in 1719.

A fine medieval bridge with refuges for

pedestrians above the cutwaters leads over a busy level crossing to **Teston**, the home of the firm of Alfred Reader, which makes cricket balls. The village cricket ground is one of those small summer idylls tucked behind the big classical manor house, Barham Court, where the house and stables have been renovated and converted into flats and offices. Next to Teston is **Wateringbury**, a once attractive village in danger of becoming part of the growing Maidstone commuter belt. A few old houses survive away from the Maidstone to Tonbridge road; one pleasing, if heavily restored, group along Mill Lane includes an 18th-century mill on a Domesday site. In summer, there are boats, and the river beside the little station becomes alive with colour and movement.

Mereworth Castle can be seen from the road west of Wateringbury, but the beautiful rooms of the house (not really a castle) are only for privileged eyes. It was England's first Palladian villa, a copy of Palladio's Villa Rotunda at Vicenza, with grand flights of steps, a big dome and a lantern that conceals 24 chimney flues. The original owner, John Fane, wanted a good view to the northern hilltop, so he simply dismantled the village of Mereworth and built it a little way to the west, with a church of 1744–6. It incorporates ideas from several London churches, and as Walpole noted, the steeple 'seems designed for the latitude of Cheapside, and is so tall that the poor church curtsies under it, like Mary Rich in a vast high-crown hat'.

Mereworth Woods to the north cover a large area, criss-crossed by paths and bridleways. Part Forestry Commission, part MoD, with a tiny corner at Gover Hill in the south-west owned by the National Trust, this is good walking and riding country. Sections of the wood are very old, probably a relic of the great Wealden forest which stretched unbroken from Canterbury to Winchester.

The Wool Trade
Until Edward III invited Flemish weavers to Kent in 1331, England was not much more than a primary producing country, standing in relation to the Continent like the Third World countries to the West today. Broadcloth was manufactured in the Weald, but it was of loosely twisted yarn and shrinkage was as much as 10 per cent. Sandwich exported mostly the raw material: in the 12 months September 1296–7 Sandwich exported 109 sacks of wool and 8563 fleeces to Flemish cloth makers. It was a long-standing grievance that the riches of the merchant princes of Bruges were enormously boosted by their trade in English wool. King Edward let it be known that 'he will grant suitable franchises to the fullers, weavers, dyers, and other cloth workers who live by this mystery, wherever such franchises were asked for'. His first substantive act was to invite a Flemish clothworker called John Kemp to settle in England. Kemp came with a group of workers to Cranbrook (which remained the centre of the Kentish cloth trade) and there taught Englishmen the arts of fulling (forcing fulling earth through cloth to carry away the grease), dyeing, weaving and milling. The Kentish trade decayed under the pressure of competition from East Anglia and was insignificant by the end of the 18th century.

North again is **Borough Green**, a commuter village beginning to stretch out towards **Ightham**. On the outskirts, close to Mereworth Woods is Great Comp, a seven-acre garden which has been designed and constructed over the last 30 years.

Beyond two motorways, **Trottiscliffe** has two nice pubs. Across a tiny green, one of them faces the weatherboarded White House, where Graham Sutherland lived in the years when, as a neo-romantic, he was influenced by the Kentish visionary period of Samuel Palmer (who lived in **Shoreham**). Just below the Pilgrims' Way is the church, quite small but crowded with visual incident. The money box in the altar rails is unique, but most extraordinary of all is the elaborate pulpit with a sounding board held aloft by a great palm tree. It was made for Westminster Abbey in 1775 and came to Trottiscliffe in 1824.

Above the church is **Trosley Country Park**, which is spelt the way the village is pronounced. Eight types of orchid grow in the turf, and other attractive flowers like rock rose can also be seen in summer. There are waymarked paths, one of them leading to the **Coldrum Stones**, the impressive remains of a Neolithic long barrow, communing across the great open space of the Medway Valley with its neighbour, **Kit's Coty**. The energetic can walk between the two.

Below the Coldrum Stones is **Addington**, with a village green, a pub, a post office, and the church a little way off. South is **Offham**, a relaxed village around a green which sports a quintain, the medieval jouster's equivalent to a prize fighter's punchball.

Nearby is **West Malling**, whose handsome High Street has recently been rescued by a bypass from the overbearing weight of traffic heading to the great depots of Paddock Wood. The church may be in one of the illustrations by Phizz for the *Pickwick Papers* (seen in the

Kit's Coty

background of the Dingley Dell versus All Muggleton cricket match). A good six-hit away is the venerable Town Malling cricket pitch where Kent used to play All-England in the days of quick under-arm bowlers.

Just south, the entrance to Manor Park country park faces the impressive bulk of St Leonard's tower, attributed to Bishop Gundulf of Rochester, and built possibly as the keep of his fortified home. In Swan Street, which leads to East Malling, is Malling Abbey, which Gundulf founded in 1090 and which was consecrated to St Mary in 1106. After the Dissolution, the abbey became a private home, but Church of England Benedictine nuns returned in 1893. The buildings vary from late-11th century to the 20th.

Eastwards the fruit farms and a small acreage of hops merge into **East Malling**, which has one foot in the big housing estates north of the A20 and M20, a consequence of post-war planning, and the other in fruit country. Bradbourne Park contains the old East Malling manor house, recased in the reign of Queen Anne with a bravura display of differently coloured and textured brick. It has a sickle-shaped lake formed by damming the trout stream, and a fine block of stables which house the library for the world-famous horticultural research station that now owns the house and park.

THE WEALD

The Medway, Teise, and Beult rivers meet in the parish of **Yalding**. The Beult is the one that runs through the spacious, green village, under a 100yds-long, narrow medieval bridge spanning the river and the marshy ground either side, with pedestrian refuges above the cutwaters. The church sits on high ground above the bridge, with a turret to one side of the tower ending in an onion-shaped cap extending into a tall weather vane. This is the

Heart Shrine
The Heart Shrine in Leybourne Church and the remains of a castle are all the barons of Leybourne (near East Malling) left behind them, though the family survived into the 20th century. When Sir Roger was killed in the Crusades his heart was brought back to the church to be enshrined. In 1286 Edward I (whose adviser he had been) and Queen Eleanor came to pay their respects and left iron crowns (still there) as offerings. The Leybournes were a remarkable family. Sir Roger's father was one of the barons who extracted the Magna Carta from King John; and Sir Roger himself was warden of the Cinque Ports. His son, Sir William, went one better, being created by Edward I England's first Admiral of the Fleet (or 'Admiral of the Sea of the King of England', as he was more grandly styled). The heart shrine has two caskets, the one on the left containing the heart of Sir Roger encased in lead. The right hand casket is solid stone and may have been meant for his wife, who married again and is buried elsewhere.

At Brabourne, another shrine probably contains the heart of John de Baliol, the founder of Balliol College, Oxford, and father of John de Baliol, King of Scotland. A second son, Alexander, lived at Chilham Castle and was a great landowner; it was he, presumably, who had his father's heart enshrined at Brabourne in 1269.

Cricket

The Postman, an 18th-century newspaper, carried an advertisement in 1705 announcing: 'This is to give notice that a match of cricket is to be plaid between 11 gentlemen of the west part of the County of Kent against as many of Chatham for 11 guineas a man at Maulden in Kent on August 7th next'. Maulden was West Malling, later to become famous in the annals of cricket as the home of Kent cricket from 1836 to 1842. Kent cannot claim absolutely to be the first county in which cricket was played, but during the 18th and 19th centuries it was the most famous home of the game, succoured and patronised as it was by the great families of Penshurst Place and Knole. An Earl of Leicester and three Sackvilles all played for Kent at Penshurst and Knole in the 18th century. Matches were often made with side stakes of between a 1,000 and 10,000 guineas, and the noble families often employed servants primarily for their cricketing abilities. The great Norfolk-born batsman Fuller Pilch became groundsman at West Malling in 1836, and Kent played and beat All England there. However, the ground was too small for the crowds needed to finance the sport. In 1842 Pilch moved to Canterbury to be joined by the 20-stone all-rounder, Alfred Mynn. They and their successor, Lord Harris, launched the game into its modern period, and saw the famous field of St Lawrence, Canterbury, established with its pavilion and tents.

heart of Kentish hop country, and when the hops are ready for harvest in late August and early September, the lanes for miles around are shaded by their height.

Nearby **Beltring** is Whitbread's hop farm, and the white cowls on its great cluster of oast houses can be seen from intercontinental jets taking off from Gatwick or heading east from Heathrow. The shire horses that pull Whitbread's drays around London take their annual holidays here, to the delight of visiting children.

The River Teise runs in a big horseshoe around **Horsmonden**. West of the village is a ¼-mile long furnace pond, once used in the Weald's iron industry. Guns were made here for both Charles I and Oliver Cromwell and the Gun Inn in the village centre has a replica of a gun made in the 17th century.

South of the village is Sprivers, a National Trust property with a garden (occasionally open) and a business in resplendent stone ornaments.

The church lies down a narrow lane two miles south-east of the village. St Margaret's only companions are a farm and a barn conversion. The church is of sandstone, lovely outside, glowing within. Inside there is a marble bust of a dyspeptic-looking John Read, the inventor of the stomach pump, who died aged 87 in 1847. The porch is almost as old as the church, sturdily built of oak with traces of carving of oakleaves in the arched braces. From the churchyard there are lovely views of the orderly husbandry of fruit and hops.

Brenchley is another pretty rural backwater that once supported 200 local men working in the iron industry. It has a lot of good and typically Wealden buildings with, at a bend in the road, a good-looking church that turns out to have been heavily rebuilt at a time when the Victorians felt they must improve on what their rude forefathers had done.

For most of its history **Matfield** was in the parish of Brenchley, so it had to wait until the 19th century to get its own version of a Decorated church. The village has grown up around the lovely green with its cricket pitch and turf roller and the big, deep red and blue brick Georgian manor, Matfield House, on one side. This is pedimented and accented by strongly articulated dormer windows and has a large clock on the stable block, inscribed beneath, 'Mind the time'. Not far away is the garden of the 17th-century Crittenden House. This is the sort of garden most of us crave, brimming with colour at all seasons. Two old ponds, more relics of the iron-working periods of the Weald, have become valuable features and, even when closed, it is possible to sample the pleasures of Crittenden simply by walking or driving past.

The cars flow through **Lamberhurst** on their way between Tunbridge Wells and Hastings, but a bypass is promised and meanwhile Lamberhurst people grit their teeth and ignore the steady rumble. The village climbs up a hill flanked by tile-hung and weatherboarded houses with one very fine timber-framed building, Coggers Hall, with a big overhang. The church is down a lane off the road to Goudhurst and has a memorial window of 1985, designed by John Piper and executed by David Wasley.

In the church the latest of the wall tablets to the Hussey family commemorates Christopher Hussey (1899–1970), editor and contributor to *Country Life*, and the lord of **Scotney Castle**, which he donated to the National Trust. The castle drive leads off the main road a ½-mile beyond the village on the way to Hastings.

The castle is on an island within a moat formed by damming the River Bewl. Only one of its heavily machicolated towers remains complete, and with its little 17th-century turret and lantern it looks no more martial than a

Scotney Castle

pepper pot. In Tudor times and through until the 18th century lords of the manor had a house amid the ruins of the castle, which various generations added to and improved. In 1837 the Husseys decided to build a new house on the hill above the castle and, quite literally, to make the castle and gardens as pretty as a picture. They sought the advice of William Sawrey Gilpin, a leading figure in the Picturesque movement. The Picturesque movement was concerned with using the landscape as a painter uses a canvas. This was done at Scotney by quarrying for rock just below the brow of the hill and above the castle. Not only did the quarry provide the building materials for the new house, it also cleared a view down to the castle moat. The new house was built in Tudor-Jacobean style, and the quarry has been absorbed into the wonderful garden. A lawn and a stone terrace with curved balustrade look over shrubs and trees and down to the castle, and during the year the scene changes as rhododendrons give way to pink calico bushes and pink and white roses that climb the castle wall, and then in high summer to buddleias, phloxes, hydrangeas, and gentians. Like all hilly places in Kent, it suffered dreadful damage during the hurricane of 1987 but has recovered wonderfully, and the gardeners have, with a touch of mordant humour, carved one massive fallen trunk into a big garden seat. When Christopher Hussey died, Henry Moore presented a little three-piece bronze figure in his memory. It reclines, beautifully, on the smaller of the two islands in the moat.

Finchcocks is easily visible from the road between Lamberhurst and Goudhurst, situated in extensive parkland and closely clasped within semi-formal walled gardens. It is reached down a ½-mile drive. The house was built in 1725, a good decade for country houses. There are many tall chimneys, one of

Mannikin at Goudhurst

them a disguised bellcote. The owners of Finchcocks have restored it and created a wonderful museum of keyboard instruments of the 17th century onwards which have been restored to playing condition. There are musical tours for visitors.

The main street of **Goudhurst** climbs from the village duckpond up a steep hill between lovely Wealden houses, to a plateau where the church tower rises to more than 500ft above sea level. It is a 17th-century late Gothic tower with a classical doorway, built to replace the original tower, which was destroyed in a storm. Like many Wealden villages, this one had an intake of Flemish weavers in the reign of Edward III, when the church was rebuilt. There are splendid monuments, especially a group for the Culpepers. The family bought the manor house of Bedgebury nearby in 1425 and lived in glory until decline and disgrace precisely two and a half centuries later, when Thomas 'Colepeper' sold the house in a vain attempt to clear his debts.

Outside the churchyard is a terrace of cottages, with one building turned end on, possibly once a bakery. In its street wall are embedded three pieces of sculpture: mannikin figures of a man and a woman (or a boy and a girl), and an urn. The urn suggests that the pieces came from the churchyard, but the figures are very unusual. Perhaps (wild guess) they are a pun on mannikin, which was the name for a kind of cloth produced in the Weald.

Due south of the village is **Bedgebury Pinetum**, a sort of living museum of conifers, our oldest class of trees. Now the national pinetum, it has several waymarked paths and rides leading to the irregularly shaped plantations of individual species spread out over two valleys and around a lake. Bedgebury gives the lie to the theory that conifers are uniformly green; in late autumn reflections

Smuggling
Heavy excise duties in the 18th century meant that there were fortunes to be made by smuggling luxuries like lace, brandy, tea and silks, in cargoes worth sometimes hundreds of thousands of pounds. An expert team could unload 500 barrels on to a moonlit beach in 20 minutes, and was powerful enough to overcome any party of excise officers sent against them. The Aldington Gang used the Walnut Tree at Aldington as their base; the Hawkhurst Gang used the Tudor Arms Inn. Churches at Snargate and Brookland were bases and hiding places, and Deal's smugglers constructed 'runs' over the rooftops, linking them with movable boards to escape the excise men. In 1784 William Pitt ordered the militia to destroy all the boats in Deal to end the problem.

There was evidently support for the smugglers, but they could be brutal. When Thomas Kingsmill, a native of Goudhurst and a leader of the Hawkhurst Gang, heard that his fellow villagers had set up a defence force, he gave them notice that on 20 April 1747 he would lead his gang into the village, slaughter the villagers, and burn Goudhurst to the ground. But one of the villagers, George Sturt, thoroughly drilled the Goudhurst Band of Militia, as they called themselves; and on the twentieth they met the Hawkhurst Gang with a withering broadside. The villagers won the day.

Timber
Look from the Downs or the greensand ridge south across the Weald and it still seems densely wooded country. For though the Weald has never been impassable, it was once thick oak and beech forest, and it remains heavily wooded, if only because those areas of heavy, poorly drained soils which were difficult to clear in the Middle Ages remain the same today. Something like 12 per cent of Kent is still woodland, which makes it one of the most heavily wooded counties in the country. The continuing supply of timber was always a matter of concern; Henry VIII and Elizabeth I passed laws to control timber felling, for oak was essential not only for the timber-framed houses of the day, but for the navy, which needed 2000 large oaks for every man o' war constructed. Sweet chestnut has become the other staple, sometimes grown to full maturity, often as a boundary marker between farms or parishes, but more usually in the chestnut coppice of the North Downs, where it is cut down every 12 or so years (its strength and flexibility is perfect for palings and hop poles) and grows again like a rampant weed. One of the great forests of England is the Bedgebury Pinetum. It is open to the public and has a wonderful range of pine, fir, redwood, yew, juniper, cypress and monkey puzzle, arranged in blocks with avenues between.

from swamp cypress and dawn redwood seem to colour the waters of the lake, while the addition of colourful deciduous trees such as *liquidambar* ensure variety along the rides.

The centre of the Wealden cloth industry was **Cranbrook**, between Goudhurst and Tenterden. When Queen Elizabeth arrived at the George on her progress through Kent in 1573, the townspeople greeted her with enthusiasm: Raleigh-like, they laid a length of Cranbrook broadcloth for her between the carriage and the front door of the inn. Today Cranbrook survives as a close-textured, busy, hilly country town with famous views of its white smock mill (still in working order) above the tiled roofs of Stone Street. The church at the top of the hill was built on the wealth made from cloth. It is beautifully light and airy, and one window is filled with 16th-century glass, probably Flemish, by craftsmen who came to England with the textile workers. The three green-man figures and a bird carved on the bosses in the chancel are all 14th century.

Benenden has an expensive but sparse feel to it. Benenden School, where Princess Anne was educated, is in a beautiful park in a mock-Elizabethan house built in the 19th century by Lord Cranbrook to replace a real Elizabethan house. There is a big church at the top of a vast sloping green, but nothing seems quite natural. In fact, most of the village was rebuilt, along with the house, by Lord Cranbrook.

Rolvenden is another village with a lovely Wealden aspect: lots of weatherboarding and a church on a hillock above the road at a bend where it dominates the scene. A lane past the church leads to Great Maytham, a big Georgian house rebuilt by Edwin Lutyens.

North of Cranbrook is **Sissinghurst Castle**. The brick tower, with its twin polygonal turrets capped by conical tiled roofs, is as brazen in the green High Weald as the clash of cymbals and the clatter of kettledrums. Only the tower survives from the original castle, where Queen Elizabeth I stayed for three nights in 1573. Her host was Richard Baker, who built the castle (really a grand manor house). After the visit, she knighted him.

Sissinghurst remained in fair condition until the 18th century when it was used to house French prisoners of war, after which it was partly demolished. When Harold Nicolson and his wife, Vita Sackville-West, saw it there was the tower, a cabbage patch, an an earlier range of buildings in front. They were enough. 'I fell in love,' she wrote later, 'Love at first sight.' Harold Nicolson worked on the drawing board, Vita Sackville-West worked in gumboots. Together they made a garden that has become one of the most famous in the world. It contains a rose garden, a cottage garden, a lime walk, a nuttery, a herb garden, an orchard (now with a gazebo in memory of Sir Harold), a right-angled moat, a yew walk, lawns, and tucked away in one corner, a little garden with clematis, Iceberg roses, *Calega Hartlandii alba*, chrysanthemums Beauté de Nivellois, lily longiflorum, snapdragons and hibiscus – the white garden.

Sissinghurst Castle

About a mile along the road to Biddenden is a pub called the Three Chimneys. It stands at the junction of three roads and the name is said to refer to the Kentish corruption of *trois chemins* (three lanes) by which the spot was known to French prisoners on exercise from Sissinghurst.

Biddenden is one of the prosperous villages of the Middle Ages that never grew but retains a lovely High Street, plenty of typical Wealden houses and the big old Cloth Hall. Inside the church tower a board commemorates a concentrated feat of change ringing on 9 April 1787: 6720 changes of Bob Major rung in 4 hours 26 minutes. A plaque in the church commemorates two local men burned at the stake in 1558 for their Protestant beliefs. More

Church Bells

Many Wealden churches have boards celebrating great feats of bell ringing, from the 18th century onwards. Biddenden has one, and at Lamberhurst on 2 May 1909 six ringers celebrated the birthday of Albert Henley, one of their number, by ringing a peal of minor for 3 hours 6 minutes: 720 each of College Single, Canterbury Pleasure and Oxford Bob; and four 720s of Plain Bob. The language and the culture of change ringing (which simply means changing the order in which the bells peal) is peculiar to the churches of the Anglo-Saxon world. Some ringers carry thousands of changes in their memories. There are around 600 churches in Kent, and 2000 church bells, in groups (called 'rings') of anything from two bells to ten; the most usual is six. In the Middle Ages itinerant bell founders cast bells in church precincts, probably in pits dug for the purpose. William le Belyeter is the first record of a Kentish founder, working in 1325, and bells made by him still ring in Canterbury, Bridge and Patrixbourne. The most famous bell in the county is Canterbury Cathedral's oldest, Bell Harry, cast by the Kentish bellfounder Joseph Hatch of Ulcombe in 1635. It weighs 8cwt and rings each weekday morning for services and every night from 8.55 to 9 for curfew, when the precinct gates are closed.

celebrated are the Biddenden Maids, Siamese twins of the 12th century who lived to 34 and left land to pay for an annual 'dole' of bread and cheese – still distributed as biscuits.

The Baby Carriage Collection at Bettenham Manor is unique to the village. Over 400 prams are shown, from 18th-century 'stickwagons' to resplendent examples of more recent times. They are housed in an oast house next to the manor, which dates from the 14th century and has a moat and a big garden.

The Pent House at **Smarden** is a cottage with a first-floor room projecting over a public right-of-way beneath into the churchyard. Inside the passage is a series of plaques commemorating all the years Smarden has won Kent's best-kept village award. The High Street (the only street), runs east to west, and sidesteps to the south of St Michael's Church. It is full of lovely houses, some timber-framed but characteristically disguising their construction with later tile-hanging; most still displaying their beams proudly, including a Wealden hall house, with wings jettied out at both ends, and another, Dragon House, whose big gable pushing out towards the road is carved with a frieze of dragons along the length of the first-floor overhang. The Cloth Hall, in Water Lane to the north of the church, is another lovely 16th-century Wealden house. St Michael's has from early times had the nickname of 'the barn of Kent'. It is built on a large scale and dates from the time when Smarden was one of the three Wealden communities licensed by Edward III to have a market.

Headcorn is a busy village, almost a small town, with a concrete silo almost on top of the High Street, a barber's shop in a wooden shed with a proper striped pole outside, a railway station and agricultural industry on the verges of the village. The shops and houses are a vivid mixture with a couple of spectacular timber-framed houses, including one called (for no good reason) Shakespeare House, with massive timbers sustaining a very high gable. Where Church Walk meets Gooseneck Lane behind the church is the pre-Reformation Headcorn Manor, not to be missed: it is a closely-studded Wealden hall house with an audacious two-storey oriel window.

The RAF Association Museum of Air Warfare is based at the still expanding Headcorn (Lashenden) Aerodrome on an old wartime site.

Pluckley declares itself to be the most haunted village in England, and lays claim to several ghosts. Whatever the truth of that, it is a pretty place in a fine position. The distinctive round-topped windows were placed there and throughout the rest of the Dering estate, by one of the Dering family. The story goes that this was to celebrate a Civil War escape through a similar window.

The Rose and Crown pub at nearby **Egerton** is always known as the Monday Boys, because, it is said, French prisoners of war were exercised in the nearby *bois* – the wood – on a Monday.

Probably more people saw the south door of **Staplehurst** church in three months in 1984 than in the first three centuries of its existence. For in those months it was removed from its hinges and placed in the Hayward Gallery in London as part of the exhibition, English Romanesque Art 1066–1200. The iron strapwork features a monstrous collection of sea-beasts, saw-edged straps of metal, and a flat-keeled Viking boat with furled sail. It is now safely back in Staplehurst village, which lies west of Headcorn and which, even more than that village, has effectively been converted to a London dormitory.

Wealden Hall Houses
The prettiest of all house types is the Wealden hall. It was built all over Kent and later spread to other counties. Typically, it has a hipped roof (sloping on all four sides), a recessed central hall, and two-storeyed wings on either side. The parlour is on the ground floor of one wing and the pantry and buttery or milkhouse is on the other. The jettied first floor contains the solar (living quarters) and bedrooms. This kind of house was built in the 14th, 15th and 16th centuries. At first, the hearth was in the middle of the hall with a hole in the roof to allow the smoke to escape. As Newcastle coal became the common fuel, the houses were built with fireplaces and chimneys; often the older houses were converted and a floor added above the hall.

There are plenty of variants on the classical type: some houses have only one jettied wing; later hall houses were erected with no jettied overhang; and in some, 18th- and 19th-century brick infill between the timbers and tile hanging often disguise the original nature of the house. Either way, the method of construction wasn't all that different from system building today. The structural timbers would be rough hewn and nailed or dowelled together and raised into position.

The Weald and Downland Open Air Museum at Singleton, West Sussex, has an example of a Wealden house.

The Channel Tunnel
The Channel Tunnel has been called the bore of the century. There have been plans to tunnel under the English Channel for nearly two hundred years. In 1870 the Ministry of Public Works reported that work in the chalk bed would be 'relatively easy and rapid'. By 1883 well over two miles of tunnel had been drilled when money ran out and public opposition overboiled. Mrs Thatcher and President Mitterrand signed the treaty for a fresh project on 29 July 1987. It was floated on privately raised capital of £6,000 million but costs soared after work had started.

The tunnel is actually two tunnels, one running each way, plus a third service tunnel. The 140 hectare British terminal is north of Folkestone. It is designed for vehicles to drive straight on to shuttle trains and for the shuttles to burrow underground between Folkestone and Dover, running under the sea beneath Shakespeare Cliff, Dover.

5 East Kent and Romney Marsh

'Does thou know Dover?' Gloucester asks as the wheel approaches full circle in Shakespeare's *King Lear*. 'Ay, sir,' says Edgar, and leads him to a cliff where:

The fishermen that walk upon the beach
Appear like mice, and yon tall anchoring bark
Diminished to her cock; her cock, a buoy
Almost too small for sight. The murmuring surge
That on th'unnumbered idle pebble chafes
Cannot be heard so high.

If Edgar could find his way with blind Gloucester today to the top of what is now known as Shakespeare Cliff, at the bottom would be no tall anchoring bark. 'Th'unnumbered idle pebble' would be buried under a promontory of excavated chalk, and though this radical distortion of land and seascape is represented by the consortium as an 'environmental opportunity', it is quite clearly a cheaper and easier solution than moving the drilled-out rock somewhere less sensitive.

For many of the people of Kent, those who

love the county, the prevailing feeling about
their situation in the face of government edict
is better represented by another of Gloucester's
lines: 'As flies to wanton boys are we to the
gods'.

Whether the balance of interest in terms of
easier travel and increased trade and prosperity
will work in the tunnel's favour can hardly be
known before the start of the 21st century.

East Kent has absorbed shocks before: but
the threat of a huge coalfield dwindled,
perhaps because the coal had to be so hard
won, and now only Betteshanger remains a
working colliery. Like the rest of Kent this
eastern region is primarily agricultural, from
the richest pasture and arable in England,
Romney Marsh, through the Quarry Hills (as
the greensand is known east of Maidstone) and
the lovely Weald folding in, at its furthest
extremity, Elham in the Nailbourne valley to
the sea- and sky-girt North Downs.

DOVER

The 13th-century chronicler Matthew Paris
described **Dover** as 'the key to England'. He
might have added that those who can't turn
the key batter down the back door. Caesar
sailed up the Dour but turned back at the sight
of the British lined up on the white cliffs on
either side and sailed to Deal instead. William
Duke of Normandy chose Hastings, but turned
east immediately after victory to consolidate
the castle of Dover. The Duke of Monmouth, in
the rebellion that led to the infamous Bloody
Assizes, chose the West Country in order to
avoid Dover and Kent; and William of Orange
followed suit. For from Caesar's day until our
own, Dover has been an armed encampment.

There was a fortification on the eastern cliffs
in Iron Age times, but the oldest building now
there is the Roman lighthouse, the Pharos.
(The equivalent pharos on the Western Heights
is not much more than a heap of rubble.) The

Constable's Tower, Dover

Dover

Population: 34,304

Early Closing: Wed

Market Day: Sat

Cashpoints: *Barclays* 21 Market Sq; *Midland* 26 Biggin St; *Nat West* 25 Market Sq, 124 High St

Tourist Information: Townwall St

Attractions: Dover Castle, Dover Museum, Old Town Gaol, Roman Painted House*

Leisure: Dover Sports Centre

By Road: London 77 miles (A2, M2), Canterbury 15 miles (A2), Folkestone 8 miles (A20)

By Rail: 1hr 30mins from London (London, Charing Cross to Dover line). Direct services to Canterbury, Folkestone and Ramsgate

By Sea: Scheduled ferry, hovercraft and jetfoil services to Belgium and France

sea came right into the broad estuary of the Dour between the eastern and western cliffs and over what is now the middle of the town. The Romans had a walled settlement on the eastern bank of the Dour (the painted house was just outside the ramparts). The timber wharf and jetty built by the Romans and rediscovered in the last few years lies somewhere beneath the bus station and multi-storey car park.

By the time the Conqueror arrived, the Saxon town was on the eastern cliff. The church of St Mary in Castro is Saxon and was the parish church of the 11th century: during the 18th century it was used as a coal store and in the 19th was restored by Sir George Gilbert Scott and decorated by Butterfield with polychrome tiles. Still, the rude brick of the chancel and nave arches is Saxon and the transept arches are Norman. The tower is over the crossing, but the Saxons had not mastered the building techniques to allow them to spread the weight through buttresses and piers, so it stands on the ground bearing its own weight, the most remarkable Kentish testimony to Saxon building techniques.

In truth the shelling and bombing of World War II have left Dover with its fair share of devastation. But the priory is still present in the name of the railway station; the great medieval pilgrims' hostel is opened up to visitors as the town's former magistrates' court and lockup; and the recently uncovered Roman painted house have been called 'the best preserved Roman paintings north of the Alps', though they are not as immediately appealing to non-specialists as the mosaics at Lullingstone; and most of the finest Roman fort found in the south of England is buried under York Street ('for future generations'). For two things Dover has no superior: the docks, which move millions of people in and out of England every year; and the castle: a fortification so secure that troops used it until 1958, and so imposing that it can be seen from France and dominates the town from any approach road.

The town itself is unendingly busy, but much pleasanter to move about in since the creation of a big pedestrian precinct in the centre, which embraces Cannon Street, where St Mary's has a lovely Norman church tower.

The Maison Dieu in Biggin Street, which was the medieval pilgrims' hostel, remains an astonishing reminder of the scale of pilgrimage: outgoing to France and Palestine, and incoming to Canterbury. The Victorian extension was by William Burges, colourfully exotic at his own home in Kensington and at Cardiff Castle, but not so here. Next door to the Maison Dieu is Maison Dieu House (the public library), a lovely 17th-century brick building with Dutch gables. Opposite is the tiny 13th-century St Edmund's Chapel, still in use. The remains of the priory are incorporated into Dover College in Effingham Crescent close by. The Roman painted house is in New Street, below modern ground level, and was preserved because 70 years after it was built in the 3rd century, the Roman defence forces built a new flint bastion straight through the middle of the house and buried it beneath an earth rampart. The paintings may be disappointing to all but archaeologists, but the ruins are highly interesting and well presented.

On the steep approach from the town to the castle stands England's most splendid and least effective gun, 24ft long, made in Utrecht in 1544 and known after the monarch to whom it was presented as 'Queen Elizabeth's pocket pistol'. Experts say that if the gun had actually been used it would probably have blown up in the faces of the gunners . . .

The castle keep is a cube of monstrously powerful proportions, 95ft high with walls more than 20ft thick and surrounded by a curtain wall with 11 towers. Henry II built it

Bleriot and Webb
An airplane modelled in concrete in a field north of Dover Castle marks the spot where Louis Bleriot landed his monoplane on 25 July 1909: the first man to fly the Channel. It was less than six years since Orville and Wilbur Wright had flown the first heavier-than-air machine, an enterprise in which the plane only skimmed the ground for a short distance. Bleriot built his craft himself, and took off from a beach south of Calais to ensure the shortest possible crossing. He was born in 1872 and lived until 1936: long enough to see HG Wells's fantastic predictions of warfare between airborne armadas come true.

The other celebrated first time crossing was by Captain Matthew Webb (born in 1848). He swam the Channel from Dover in 21¾ hours in 1875. Hundreds of swimmers have followed since, including an 11-year-old boy, and some have swum both ways. Matthew Webb drowned in 1883 attempting to swim the rapids above Niagara Falls.

Ashford

Population: 45,962

Early Closing: Wed

Market Days: Tue, Sat

Cashpoints: *Barclays* 66 High St; *Midland* 39 High St; *Nat West* 20 High St

Tourist Information: Lower High St

Attractions: Godinton Park* (2½m NW), Intelligence Corps Museum (open only by appointment)

Leisure: Stour Centre

Cinema: Picture House

By Road: London 55 miles (A20, M20), Folkestone 16 miles (M20), Canterbury 14 miles (A28)

By Rail: 1hr from London (London, Charing Cross to Folkestone line). Direct services to Canterbury, Folkestone, Hastings, Maidstone and Sevenoaks

and the inner bailey surrounded by the inner curtain wall. He also built part of the outer curtain wall, with flanking towers projected forward from the walls to give a clear field for raking fire upon anyone coming close enough to try to scale them. There are two wonderful Romanesque chapels within the keep. The whole cost to the exchequer was £7,000. The annual budget of the kingdom was £10,000.

Henry II's son King John carried the work forward, but he fell out with his barons and in 1216 they invited the French king, Louis, to take the crown. Louis's troops undermined the northern gate and only the fighting skills of Hubert de Burgh's men, holding the castle for John, enabled them to hold out. After this unnerving experience the castle was strengthened by blocking the northern gate with a third tower between the twin gatehouse bastions (hence the tripled Norfolk towers now), and outworks including a couple of towers (St John's Tower still standing) reached by the underground tunnels. During the Napoleonic Wars the towers were cut down and levelled as gun platforms. What remains is forbiddingly impressive in its bulk and deeply fascinating in detail. On the Western Heights there are fortifications built in the Napoleonic scare. Further on is Shakespeare Cliff, with wonderful views, though not for the blinded Gloucester in *King Lear*, who came here to throw himself into oblivion. Inland on the A2 is Kent's second motor racing circuit at Lydden Hill, small, friendly, and still used by the BARC for meetings.

ASHFORD

Ashford is a place where roads meet, and the centre is most easily understood as an island containing High Street, East Hill, Middle Row, North Street, New Street, and the big parish church. It was always a meeting of the roads, from Folkestone, Maidstone, Canterbury,

Tenterden and Lydd. It waxed and grew fat on
its roads. As a market town it was second to
none. And what is most worth seeing today is
on the island: rich Georgian houses, jettied
half-timbered buildings, some nice pargeting,
and some lovely tile-hanging. Best of all is a
delightful group of town houses and the old
red-brick grammar school of 1635–6 which hem
the churchyard in with only a pavement
between them.

Ashford is still bustling and prosperous and
some say bullying: its council is responsible for
Tenterden and in recent years has been trying
to impose its style of planning on to Tenterden
against strong local opposition. In Ashford the
handsome Perpendicular church tower with its
four tall pinnacles, each topped with a golden-
arrow weathervane, holds its own against the
bingo hall, the massive Girobank office block,
and the supermarkets which one can't help
feeling might have been better placed
elsewhere.

On the north-west outskirts, topiary hedges
clasp the garden close to the bosom of the
house at Godinton Park. The house started life
as a Wealden half-timbered hall-house, but
when Captain Toke came into his inheritance
in 1627 – in the intervals between marrying
five wives – he transformed it. It is, despite the
late date, basically Jacobean, with gables like
Knole's. There are fireplaces of the local
Bethersden marble and the sumptuous
panelled rooms, elaborately carved with
varying degrees of skill but great vitality by
local craftsmen, contrast with the rooms
installed by the 20th-century owners: pale and
elegant, and filled with Chippendale mirrors
and chairs, Sheraton, Louis XV; Sèvres china,
Worcester, Dresden and lovely Chelsea
pottery.

Close to the A20 is **Hothfield Common**, a
nature reserve and a Site of Special Scientific
Interest. More than 60 species of birds have

been recorded here in an unusual Kentish example of heath and bog habitat. Some of the plants in the boggy areas are quite rare but are easily studied from the causeway which forms part of the two-mile figure-of-eight nature trail.

Charing slumbers peacefully as the traffic divides at the roundabout a few yards west of the village and speeds by on the main roads to Canterbury and Dover. But in Charing, the Pilgrims' Way turns north and climbs the Downs for the last leg of the route to Canterbury. Here was the last of the three Archbishop's palaces along the Pilgrims' Way. Archbishop Warham entertained Prince Henry there in 1507 and was host again when Henry VIII stopped overnight in 1520 on his way to the Field of the Cloth of Gold. Today the ruined gatehouse opens on to a farm yard, and the great hall of 1340 does duty as a barn. The farmhouse itself is a flint and brick building extended in 1586 from a 12th-century house.

The church has a roof beam elaborately carved with fronds. Between the church and the vicarage is a great yew tree to which was fixed a stone plaque in 1772 commemorating:

an once brave soldier and honest gentleman Joshua Marshall Esqr. He was father of a vicar of this Parish . . . O Vicar, whoever thou art reflect and profit by the reflexion how small the distance and perhaps quick the transition from yon house thou inhabitest to the caverns of the dead.

Tree of Jesse window, Westwell

Church and palace are along a lane that runs at right angles from the High Street about halfway up. The High Street itself climbs up the gentle lower slopes of the North Downs and is flanked by a lovely collection of traditional houses, shops and pubs. Another lane leads eastwards into some of the quietest and most beautiful pastoral landscape in the county to **Westwell**: a few houses among big plane trees and beeches, a group of horse chestnuts on a small triangular green, a couple of peacocks wandering out of a barnyard and across the road, and a modern rectory opposite the church, where the vicar keeps a key to the church big enough to unlock the kingdom of heaven.

The church of St Mary may not be that, but the interior emphatically gives the lie to the exterior. Almost the first thing you see inside are great timber buttresses in the south aisle holding up the arcade at the east end of the nave and west of the chancel where it tilts alarmingly outwards. The cause of this is the simple but splendid stone rib vault in the chancel; the stone screen in the chancel arch is also remarkable and one lancet window has a complete 13th-century Jesse tree (showing the ancestry of Jesus); or rather, the top half is complete, the bottom half was reconstructed in 1960 by a Canterbury craftsman using fragments of medieval glass.

The lane leads on past Eastwell Park, with a big Victorian neo-Jacobean gatehouse full of sound and fury. The house has been pulled down and replaced with a hotel. Beyond the Stour Valley is **Wye**, 'a well-haunted market' in Lambarde's time; still small-scale, mostly Georgian around the High Street though with a spreading outskirt of housing estates. Wye College is the agricultural college of London University, but it is built around the nucleus of the 15th-century college founded by the Archbishop of Canterbury, John Kempe, who, to quote Lambarde again, was 'the childe of a poore husbande man in Wye' but rose to be a cardinal.

An agricultural museum has been set up by the college, and the bulk of the collection of farm equipment is preserved in a fine, black-weatherboarded 14th-century barn which housed the tithes for Christ Priory, Canterbury. The exhibits range from large items like haywagons and harvesters to smaller implements and hand tools, many of them

The Downs
There are the North Downs, high and dry, and the Downs, which is the name of a comparatively sheltered anchorage for ships. As Julius Caesar was the first to find out in twice losing his boats in that 'Purgatorio of the high seas', (as the Kentish poet Richard Church put it) the shelter is only comparative. It is provided by the Goodwin sands, six miles out and clearly visible at low tide, and marked by four lightships. But as vessels and fleets became bigger, the Downs were used more and more by British shipping. Here Charles II's ship rode at anchor when he returned to claim the throne of England in April 1660 and here Nelson's body lay aboard the *Victory* for three days after the Battle of Trafalgar. It is said that sometimes you can hear the muffled tolling of church bells from the Goodwins, which in the 12th century were the lands of the Earl of Godwin. A likely story – but it does say something about the changing characteristics of the Kent coastline over the centuries.

Julius Caesar's Landing
Historians always say that Gaius Julius Caesar landed at Deal in the autumn of 55 BC on his first reconnaissance of Kent, and on the sea front at Deal today is a plaque recording Caesar's arrival. Yet because there was no settlement here Caesar himself never names the landing place. Still, the clarity of Caesar's report on the expedition in his account *The Conquest of Gaul* (*De Bello Gallico*) gives the clearest possible indication. The expedition was organised on the basis of the deepest ignorance. Caesar didn't know the nature of the terrain, he didn't know the fighting methods of the native Belgae, he didn't even know the best landing places. He opted to take the shortest route (or nearly; there was a Roman port at Boulogne and this was the probable departure point). But when Caesar arrived he found the British lining the cliffs where 'javelins could be hurled from the cliffs right on to the narrow beach enclosed between them and the sea'. So, after giving time for the rest of the fleet to catch up, Caesar 'gave the signal for weighing anchor, and after sailing for about seven miles ran his ships aground on an evenly sloping beach'. As nearly as possible, that pinpoints the stretch of beach from Kingsdown through Walmer to Deal; and the 'high ground' on which the British are said to have remained out of sight during the following year's expedition suggests Deal itself.

made and used locally.

The road climbs out of Wye to **Wye and Crundale Downs**, lined with people gazing through binoculars over Romney Marshes and beyond Hythe, and as the road crosses Stone Street (the Roman road, straight as an arrow, between Lympne and Canterbury) and turns north, there are more extensive views, this time to the Richborough cooling towers and beyond to Pegwell Bay. The big attraction of the Downs here is the nature reserve with carefully protected orchids, including some rarities, butterflies, rare or typical of chalk downland, birds and dramatic features like the Devil's Kneading Trough, a coombe in the chalk.

At **Upper Hardres**, there is an interesting little Norman and Early English church (key next door). Further north-east, across the main Canterbury to Dover road, **Patrixbourne** also has a Norman church, with a fine carved tympanum, which tends to be overlooked in favour of Barfreston's. The pretty village was the home of Count Zborowski, one of the racing drivers and miniature railway enthusiasts who dreamt up the Romney, Hythe and Dymchurch Railway.

Close by is **Bekesbourne**, where John Aspinall runs Howletts, one of his two great animal collections in Kent. This one has the world's largest captive gorilla colony, and at *Port Lympne* (see below), the animals are given plenty of space.

From Patrixbourne to Elham the villages lie along the charming Nailbourne valley. This is one of Kent's 'intermittent' streams, not always there, and also called 'woe waters' because of the havoc their flash floods bring. Beyond Littlebourne it flows as a normal stream, and becomes the Little Stour.

West again of the main road, **Bishopsbourne** is cupped in a little green valley: it was home for the last five years of his life (1919-24) to

Joseph Conrad and cannot have changed much since. The church has a window by Burne-Jones, with pale and wan Pre-Raphaelite figures and fruit trees behind, full of colour.

Bourne Park and its grounds are not open to the public, but are well worth looking at from the road: an idyll of an English 18th-century country house.

Three or four miles south-east **Barham** lies just to the side of the road through the Nailbourne valley, another cluster of 18th-century brick houses and barns on a hill, all overtopped by the church and with another big 18th-century country house, tucked in behind the church, and with a formidable gatehouse by Lutyens.

Elham is the culmination of the road along the valley of the Nailbourne, and the culmination of its High Street is a big timber-framed inn of 1614 with the overhanging first floor beams carried on a series of vividly grotesque Hieronymus Bosch-like caryatids. There are more carvings within. East of the High Street, a neat little square is closed to the south by the church, which has exotic Edwardian (and later) restoration work: canopiesin scarlet, blue and gold, and a polychrome St George slaying a humanoid dragon.

At the southern end of the Roman Stone Street, **Lympne** is reached. The paltry remains of Roman Lympne, Portus Lemanis, lie at the foot of the cliff. Lympne church and castle are excitingly placed on top of the cliff and make a fine group. The castle is really a fortified manor house, modernised as recently as 1905. The gardens give good views. Nearby is **Port Lympne Zoo**, one of John Aspinall's two zoo parks in Kent (the other is Howletts at Bekesbourne). The animals include elephants, wolves, rhinos and antelopes, and various big cats. Walks of different lengths are suggested, and sometimes 'safari trails' are offered. The

Port Lympne Zoo

house and the elaborate gardens (much helped
by elephant dung) are also open. Back towards
Ashford, the Walnut Tree at **Aldington**
overlooks Romney Marsh and is linked with
the unpleasant Ransley or Aldington gang of
smuggling fame. Ford Madox Huefer (later
Ford) lived here, and in 1511 the Dutch
humanist Erasmus was the rector.

South of **Mersham** is Swanton Mill, with a
pretty garden. The mill was restored from
dereliction in 1969, and now grinds corn again
– the only mill in Kent to do so – and sells the
flour. In the church at Mersham is a wide
window with the 12 apostles side by side; less
famous but more satisfying is a 12th-century
lancet in the church at **Brabourne**: an
interlocking pattern of flowers in pink, yellow,
ochre, grey, brown, green, and brilliant ruby
red.

DEAL
Medieval Deal was on high ground above
today's seaside town, but the Downs (the
channel between Deal and the Goodwin
Sands) was sheltered from the worst of the
English Channel's storms by the shallows of
the Sands, and became an important
anchorage. A busy maritime community grew
up ashore. 'A very pitiful town', Samuel Pepys
declared Deal to be when he arrived from the
Netherlands with Charles II's fleet at the
Restoration; but the new town had been built
when Celia Fiennes visited in 1697 and
admired the 'neate brickwork' and the
gardens. Deal remains a 17th-century town of
pretty sea-front houses with narrow lanes of
brick and stuccoed cottages, white- and pink-
washed, running east to west between the sea
front and the High Street. There are boats
bright as paintboxes on the shingle beach.
Only the concrete pier jars. Maybe it was built
to withstand the impact of ill-directed
shipping: the last iron and timber pier was

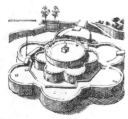

Deal Castle

mown down in 1940 by a Dutch vessel that had hit a mine and was adrift. Almost opposite the pier is Time Ball Tower, with a big red ball that drops from top to bottom of a shaft atop the building at one o'clock each afternoon. Now Time Ball Tower is a museum of time, telegraphy and communications. North of the pier is the Maritime Museum with several examples of the historic Deal 'beach boats'.

Deal may drop to sleep from time to time, but it is all there. During World War II it was not just bombed but shelled and torpedoed as well. Its boats were in the frontline of the Dunkirk rescue: of ten that left Deal, three were sunk, one on its fifth trip to Dunkirk. In 1946 the mayor unveiled a plaque on the sea front south of Deal Castle recording Deal's first distinguished visitor 2,000 years before, Julius Caesar. In the years since 55 BC Deal has usually been in some state of preparation for war.

Henry VIII's defences included, in only a couple of miles of Deal's coastline, three of the best castles contemporary technology could deliver: more like compact 20th-century machine-gun pillboxes than the medieval castles of Tonbridge or Leeds, shaped like a many-leafed clover to give a wide field of fire and to deflect enemy missiles. The one north of the town at Sandown has succumbed to time and tide, but its tiny remnant has been shored up as a bulwark against further incursions of the sea and does duty as a rock garden. Deal Castle sits behind its moat only a couple of hundred yards from the town pier. This was the home of the captain of Deal Castle until World War II, when the army gave him 24 hours to pack his bags. Probably just as well: the enemy scored a direct hit on his living quarters soon afterwards. Otherwise it looks as businesslike now as the day it was built.

In sharp contrast behind a screen of tall trees **Walmer Castle** hardly looks like a sister

The Coalfield
It could be a small colliery town, with the gauntly skeletal winding gear, the waste tips, the village shop, the rows of cottages and the canteen. Yet down the hill are hop gardens and fields of wheat and turnips. This is Betteshanger in East Kent, west of Deal, the last surviving colliery in the county. Professor RAC Godwin-Austen was years ahead of his time when he suggested in 1855 that the coalfields of northern France probably extended under the sea into Kent. The first pit, at Snowdown, did not open until 1913. Tilmanstone followed quickly, then Betteshanger and Chislet. From then on there was coal fever; the national interest was perceived to override local interest and a Kentish coalfield of 250 square miles was enthusiastically proposed, with an overhead conveyor belt from Tilmanstone to bunkers at Dover. Miners came from all parts during the Depression, and Betteshanger colliery rugby team still sports an array of Davieses and Joneses indistinguishable from a South Wales valley 15. With the increasing commitment to other forms of fuel, Tilmanstone was closed in October 1986 and Snowdown a year later. Betteshanger continues, producing around 10,000 tons of top-grade coking coal a week.

Holy Maid
One of the more bizarre victims of the Reformation in England was the so-called Holy Maid of Kent, Elizabeth Barton (1506–34). She was a servant girl on the estates of the Archbishop of Canterbury at Aldington, above the Romney Marshes, who was epileptic and prone to visions. A monk of Canterbury, Edward Bocking, either agreed with the prevailing opinion that she was possessed of the Holy Ghost or used her as an instrument in the propaganda war against reformers. She performed the requisite miracles, was taken to Canterbury and impressed Archbishop Warham and others who should have known better, like Bishop John Fisher and Sir Thomas More. A visit to her cell at Canterbury became almost as great a popular attraction as Becket's shrine. But when the king announced his intention of divorcing Catherine of Aragon and marrying Anne Boleyn, Elizabeth Barton first foretold that he would 'die a villain's death' and then burst in on him with Cassandra-like intensity when he passed through Canterbury. Her dismal fate was assured. Cranmer cross-examined her at Otford. She was arrested soon after, and she, Edward Bocking, the Aldington parish priest, and the warden and former warden of Greyfriars, Canterbury, who had publicised her early miracles, were all executed in London.

fortification. Walmer Castle is the official residence of the Warden of the Cinque Ports. Once this was the Duke of Wellington. No one ever thought to give him notice to quit. He died in residence and his is the presiding spirit, even though his successors included Winston Churchill (who never took up residence) and the Queen Mother. The Duke's bedroom has been preserved as it was when he lived and died there: sparsely, that is, with his folding camp bed, his shaving mirror and not a lot more. The garden is a sheer delight, laid out originally by Lady Hester Stanhope (when her uncle William Pitt the Younger lived in the castle) with lawns, flower beds and great fig trees clinging to the walls.

St Leonard's Church, on the way out to Sandwich in Upper Deal among a group of Georgian houses, runs, naturally, west to east; but from outside it looks as though it runs north to south. This is because not only does the original Norman nave have two side aisles, but in 1819 a north annexe was added with a gallery and porch. The chancel has a 12th-century piscina and there is another of the 15th-century in the south aisle chapel. Above the nave is a craftsmanlike gallery built by the pilots of Deal in 1705 and used now for the organ. With its white cupola on a square tower it is altogether unusual and unusually delightful.

West of Deal is the half-lost village of **Barfreston**, where Romanesque art became naturalised by its English setting. Nothing could be less like the sunny Romanesque art of Lombardy and Burgundy. The church of St Nicholas is under 50ft long, but packs in a fantastic menagerie of birds and beasts and mythical creatures around its walls. On the three orders of arches and the shafts and voussoirs there are knights jousting, archers, a woman filling a goatskin from a barrel, more animals, a battling centaur, a man threshing and lions fighting dragons: a rich stone tapestry of the daily round, the tales around the hearth, and the nightly dream. On the east wall there are still more fantastic carvings.

The male crowned head in the tympanum has bulging eyes, which confirms for some historians that these heads are portraits of Henry II and his queen, Eleanor of Aquitaine, who were on the throne when the church was built. At the apex of the doorway is a figure of a bishop, who may be Becket. There are signs that this was introduced at a late stage. (Although Becket was murdered in 1170 when Barfreston was still being built, the south door may well have been complete by then and would have needed to be altered for this stop press item.)

The village is small and built into a steep hollow. Just above the church is Jasmine Cottage, which Henry Moore bought for £80 in 1931 and where he lived and worked during the period of his early maturity in the 1930s.

St Margaret's Bay is clasped by the indentation of the white cliffs just north of the South Foreland and is reached by steeply inclined S-bends. It is worth it. The beach is small and pebbled, the cliff is wooded and has a path leading south-west along the cliffs to Dover. It is quiet, and a good place to picnic and watch the passing show of Channel ships.

Barfreston church

The National Trust owns much of the land on the cliffs and the Saxon Shore Way here runs over the cliffs between Deal and Dover (not strictly part of the Shore which the Romans defended against the Saxons). There is a very pleasant circular walk from St Margaret's to Kingsdown along the coast, returning inland, and another towards the Langdon Cliffs picnic site with fine views of the ferry terminal. The return journey, again inland, totals about 6 miles.

St-Margaret's-at-Cliffe has a big Norman church with a richly carved west doorway of around 1150 embraced in a large triangular

Folkestone

Population: 43,998

Early Closing: Wed

Market Days: Thu, Sun

Cashpoints: *Barclays* 65/67
Sandgate Rd; *Lloyds* 43
Sandgate Rd; *Midland* 41
Sandgate Rd; *Nat West* 2
Castle Hill Ave, 49
Sandgate Rd

Tourist Information:
Harbour St

Attractions: Eurotunnel
Interpretation Centre (St
Martin's Plain, Cheriton
High St), Museum and Art
Gallery

Arts: Leas Cliff Hall,
Metropole Arts Centre

Leisure: Amusement Park;
Folkestone Sports Centre
and Ski Centre

By Road: London 71 miles
(M20, A20), Canterbury 16
miles (A260, A2), Dover 8
miles (A20)

By Rail: 1hr 20mins from
London (London, Charing
Cross to Folkestone line).
Direct services to Ashford,
Dover, Ramsgate and
Sevenoaks. Connections to
Canterbury and Hastings
via Ashford

By Sea: Scheduled ferry
services to France

gable shape that is also sculpted with figures
and abstract patterning. The north doorway,
within a later porch, is Norman as well, but
less elaborate. Inside there are impressively
massive and matching chancel and tower
arches and a clerestory arcade pierced with a
window in every third arch. A new window
inserted early in 1988 commemorates the three
men of the village who died in the sinking of
the *Herald of Free Enterprise* at Zeebrugge the
year before.

FOLKESTONE

The railway came to Folkestone in 1843 – over
William Cubitt's spectacular viaduct – and the
population increased seven times from 4,400 to
more than 30,000 by the end of the century.
Down by the harbour the shopping streets still
have the configuration of the fishing village it
was; but none of the buildings is pre-Victorian.
In Defoe's day Folkestone was 'eminent chiefly
for a multitude of fishing boats belonging to it,
which are one part of the year employ'd in
catching mackarel for the city of London'. But
if the holidaymakers brought true prosperity to
Folkestone, it is the port which now sustains it.

At Marine Parade west of the harbour there
is a big funfair, and beside the harbour a big
hotel, but the fashionable no longer come to
Folkestone. The great Victorian hotels are not
what they were: the New Metropole is an arts
centre, which is ultimate proof that there is no
money in it any more. Still, the Leas remain
quintessential Folkestone. It is a promenade
with a wide stretch of lawn, the perfect place
for studying the French coast and Channel
shipping at leisure. There are terraces of big
cream-stuccoed houses; a bandstand that ought
to have blown away on the first decent sea
breeze; tall lamp posts with cast-iron tendrils of
foliage and effetely drooping heads festooned
with flowers in hanging baskets and strings of
light bulbs which throw a gentle glow over the

cliff top as evening draws in; and the Leas Pavilion, which looks as though it has been carved from a big bar of yellow soap, its name picked out in white on the apron of a glass canopy. A block of modern flats has replaced one of the terraces. It is in concrete and white brick with glass screens shielding the balconies – good, but definitely not at home with the crinoline culture that begot the Leas.

On the cliffs east of the town are three of the coastal range of Martello towers built against the Napoleonic threat. Immediately beyond them are the chalk cliffs of the Warren, arguably the best place in southern England for studying migrant butterflies and moths. A little behind the town is the old RAF fighter station of **Hawkinge**, quite literally the front line of defence in the Battle of Britain and in range of German guns on the French coast. Today it houses a museum containing Britain's largest collection of recovered fragments of aircraft involved in the battle.

To the west Folkestone merges with **Sandgate**, where another four Martello towers coexist with one of the castles (not open) built by Henry VIII to the same plan as Deal and Walmer, but reduced in status and size in 1806 to no more than a gun battery like the Martello towers. A copy of the accounts for the original design and building in 1539–40 is displayed in Deal Castle: Henry employed the German military engineer Stephan von Haschenperg (who was later fired amid recriminations about misapplication of funds), and the total cost to the exchequer was £5,543 19s 2¾d.

Martello tower, Folkestone

ROMNEY MARSH

Tenterden was both port and wool town. Its church and the handsome houses in the High Street proclaim its ancient prosperity. Buildings of the 15th, 16th and 17th century glow orange and white along the High Street. There is a town hall of 1780 with a first floor jettied out on pillars over the pavement, like Deal's, but crisper, with a Venetian Gothick central window. Further east the ensemble relaxes and widens to allow grass and trees with detached houses on the north and a row of low weatherboarded shops on the south.

North of the High Street is Tenterden railway station which once linked with the main line at Headcorn. In earlier times it was a great hop-pickers' line, but it closed in the 1950s. Within 10 years, enthusiasts had begun the task of restoring it and relaying sections of the track which had been lost. Now the Kent and East Sussex Railway pursues a more leisurely route south and west towards Northiam, with dinner served on certain evenings in the summer.

South-east, the road leads out to Romney Marsh through **Smallhythe**, once the port of Tenterden. The Tudor harbour master's house is known to us as the last home of Ellen Terry and now a museum of her memorabilia. Further south, at **Wittersham**, is Stocks Mill, a good place to get to grips with the mechanics and construction of a post mill. It was designed to be easily dismantled and portable.

Once it is quite clear that most of Romney Marsh is as much as 10ft below sea level with nothing very obvious keeping the sea out, that Dungeness is growing so perceptibly into the Channel that it has left four lighthouses behind it, that when the bible speaks of the shepherd and his flock the church builders of the Marsh seem to have taken it literally, and that the port of Tenterden is a good 10 miles from the sea; once all this is clear everything else falls into place. As the man says in Kipling's *Puck of Pook's Hill*, 'I've heard say the world's divided like into Europe, Ashy, Africky, Ameriky, Australy, an' Romney Marsh'. It is a remote place, once much used by smugglers ('brandy for the parson . . . baccy for the clerk,' wrote Kipling), who appear to have been

Romney Marsh – marsh frog

given plenty of help by local people.

In 1803 William Pitt the Younger caused the Royal Military Canal to be dug from below Winchelsea to Hythe. Covered with lilies, with sheep grazing safely on the banks and with anglers dozing in the sunshine, it looks innocuous enough. William Cobbett could hardly contain his indignation at the funds its construction consumed, and the hovels the farm labourers lived in, and at the very notion that a general whose armies had forded the Rhine would be held up by a canal. He might have been right. With the wind at your back, you could spit across the canal.

The canal lies just outside **Appledore**. Cross it and you are into the Marsh. Appledore's ship-building and wool-based prosperity shows in its street of warm orange brick-and-tile houses and white and brown timber and plaster. There was a French raid in 1380 – overland, because Appledore had lost its natural moorings in the great storm of 1287 that so changed the landscape and the economy. From Appledore, you can walk along the Royal Military Canal towards Hamstreet. You will be sampling another section of the 140-mile long Saxon Shore Way from Gravesend to Rye, last seen at St Margaret's-at-Cliffe. The route leaves the canal near Warehorne and passes close to the Nature Reserve at **Ham Street Woods** – a large wood on the edge of the marshes which contains many classic old woodland trees including oak, hazel and sweet chestnut. Britain's largest and most elusive finch, the hawfinch, can sometimes be heard or glimpsed flitting through the hornbeam of the wood. Nightingales are summer residents in the reserve. From here it would be possible to return to Appledore, or continue along the South Saxon Way to Lympne.

There are other good walks to be had under the wide skies of the marsh, and it can be

William Caxton

Tenterden claims William Caxton (around 1422–91) as its son, though even the latest studies, timed to coincide with the 500th anniversary of printing in England, adduce no new evidence. Caxton himself said that he was a native of the Weald of Kent, born into a family which originated in the neighbourhood of Hadlow: Tenterden is entirely feasible, since it was a wool town and a port. As soon as he left school Caxton was sent by his father as an apprentice to a member of the Mercer's Company in the City of London. The main dealings of the mercers were through the great trading city of Bruges, and it was to Bruges that Caxton went to set up in business on his own account. Caxton had been well schooled in Kent ('I am bounded to pray for my fader and moder's souls,' he wrote in the preface to one of the books printed on his press later, 'that in my youthe sent me to schoole, by which by the suffraunce of God, I gete my living, I hope truly'), and during his travels from Bruges to Utrecht and Cologne he became more and more fascinated by literary pursuits. Either in Cologne or Bruges he learnt the rudiments of printing and in 1474 printed and published a translation of a French romance, *The Recuyell of the Historyes of Troye*. Two years later Caxton returned home and set up the first English printing press in the precincts of Westminster Abbey.

The Cinque Ports
The Cinque Ports
(pronounced 'sink' but a
corruption of the French
cinq) were a confederation
of coastal towns owing ship
service to the king. The
allegiance dates back before
records began, and was
certainly well established at
the time of Edward the
Confessor, when Dover
owed 'to the king, once in
the year, twenty ships for
fifteen days, and in each
ship were twenty-one
men'. The other four
Cinque Ports were
Hastings, New Romney,
Hythe and Sandwich, to
which were added later the
'antient towns' of Rye and
Winchelsea.

Before the Norman
Conquest it was probably a
loose alliance, including a
number of other towns
called 'limbs'; afterwards it
became an institution, with
the right of 'sac and soc' (to
hold courts and to keep the
fines), and even later the
right to dry their nets on
the beach at Yarmouth and
sell catches there without
paying tax. This became a
running sore exacerbated
when the Yarmouth
(Norfolk) and Cinque Ports
elements of the king's fleet,
on its way to Sluys in 1297,
quarrelled and the Cinque
Ports sailors destroyed 32
Yarmouth ships and killed
200 men.

Today only Dover is still
a port. But there remains a
Lord Warden in charge of
jurisdiction (a nominal post)
and 18 'coronation barons'
still represent the Cinque
Ports at the Coronation,
though they no longer raise
a canopy over the
monarch's head.

wonderfully bleak. There are some public
footpaths, and there is so little traffic, except in
the high season, that walking along the minor
roads is perfectly pleasant. The most famous
means of transport in the area is the Romney,
Hythe and Dymchurch Railway (see *New
Romney*), but for seeing the churches of the
Marshes the best way is to drive or cycle. Often
isolated, always idiosyncratic, the churches
form an unparalleled group. Little restored for
the most part, they show how very many more
churches would have looked if the Victorians
had not been such enthusiastic rebuilders.
They also show how prosperous the area used
to be, when its little towns were among the
Cinque Ports, and had all the privileges that
went with the job of defending the coast, until
the sea moved away.

Driving across the Marsh you can always
see the semi-circle of high ground to the north
that was once the coastline of a great bay: not
120 million years ago when the geological
structure of Kent was laid down; nor 250,000
years ago, when Swanscombe man hunted on
the chalk near Gravesend; nor even 8,000 years
ago, when the sea divided Kent from the
Continent. Romney Marsh was under the sea
in historical times: as recently as 1538 Henry
VIII visited Smallhythe to inspect one of his
warships under construction. The Isle of Oxney
was an island; Rye sat on a small islet; so did
Winchelsea. As Roman, Saxon, Norman and
Plantagenet successively reclaimed land from
the sea, Lydd grew up on an island three or
four miles out to sea behind the shingle
promontory of Denge Ness. Roman Lympne,
Portus Lemanis, was at the end of a creek. Old
Romney and its church sat on a little island.
The road from Appledore to New Romney
runs along the top of the great, ancient
earthwork known as the Rhee Wall,
constructed to stop the channel along which
the Rother at one time ran from flooding the

Marsh. New Romney, one of the Cinque Ports, lay at the point where the Rother spilled into the sea, and ships tied up to the church wall.

Then the cataclysmic storm of 1287 altered the geography and the economy of the area. The alluvial soils of the Marsh were no kind of defence against the gales and hurricanes that struck that year, and overnight the winds diverted the Rother to Rye. Once the floods had subsided, Romney was stranded a mile from the sea. To this day the marks of the flooding are visible on the great Norman pillars inside New Romney church.

Romney Marsh fattened sheep better than any other area of England or Wales; it was the basis for the success of the wool trade of the Weald, and Tenterden waxed fat on the wool of Romney Marsh. This is good arable land as well, and there have always been crops. Today there are more than ever, but the flocks remain, 'very pretty and large,' as William Cobbett remarked as he rode by on his way to Dover in 1823. 'The faces of these sheep are *white*; and, indeed, the whole sheep is as white as a piece of *writing paper*. The wool does not look dirty and oily like that of other sheep.' Romney Marsh sheep (or 'Kents') are a hardy breed too: they helped form the huge flocks of Australia. Their shepherds (called 'lookers') once had little huts on the marshes in summer; in winter, the flocks moved inland, when, in the words of E H Carrier, writing in 1936, 'the bleating of the ovine troops fills the countryside.'

The Dungeness peninsula is the part of the Marsh where no sheep will ever fatten. A map may show which is **Greatstone** and which is **Littlestone**, but as you leave New Romney in search of the sea that departed so suddenly 700 years ago, the two resorts merge identities in an unbroken line of well-loved villas putting down roots in much the same way as the patches of gorse and foxglove that somehow

Dungeness

sustain themselves on nothing but shingle. People retire here, people holiday here, and some of the fishermen live here, crunching over the shingle in their morning seaboots to shove their boats into the waves, coming back early in the afternoon with their catches and chalking up on blackboards what they have to offer to the passing world.

Then, at the tip of **Dungeness** these buildings give way to do-it-yourself houses displaying a wide range of ingenuity and wit. These bungalows are adapted from old water towers, railway carriages, bits of greenhouse, garden trellis, bedsteads and corrugated iron. Telephone wires are draped like droopy washing lines across the landscape; the landscape itself is flatter than the sea, but not featureless exactly, because the backdrop to this metamorphosis of junk into ideal homes is serried ranks of monstrous six-armed pylons marching northwards from two vast complexes of glass and concrete and pipes known as Dungeness A and Dungeness B nuclear power stations. One reason for siting the power stations here is that they need vast quantities of water to cool the reactors. And, of course, the rate of growth of the shingle promontory into the English Channel is not going to make any measureable difference until long after nuclear power has become obsolete.

Saltwood Castle

But it has made a difference to the merchant marine. The first lighthouse in Dungeness, lit by a great coal fire, was built in 1615. By 1635 it was too far inland to be much use so a second was built. In 1792 Samuel Wyatt built the third; by 1904 a fourth lighthouse was needed. It was built 136ft high, but by 1960 the glow from Dungeness drowned the million candlepower illumination thrown out from the great reflectors, and a fifth lighthouse became necessary. Its light can be seen 27 miles out to sea and for the moment this is deemed to be sufficient. Certainly the light is sufficient for the migrant birds, butterflies and moths which use it as a landmark, arriving in their thousands each spring and autumn. The RSPB have had a reserve here since the 1930s.

At the eastern approach to the Marsh, and not strictly of the Marsh but the end of the Military Canal, sits **Hythe**, which means landing place. It is another of the Cinque Ports stranded by silting far from the sea. The attractive High Street with its 18th-century town hall lies at the foot of a steep hill; St Leonard's Church is at the top and is a stirring sight from the Folkestone road. It has one of the finest chancels in a parish church anywhere, thanks to 13th-century prosperity. The crypt is full of ancient skulls and bones, and is the big tourist attraction.

Halfway back to the High Street is Centuries, at the end of St Bartholomew's road. This ancient house was the birthplace of Bishop Hamo de Hythe, whose tomb is in Rochester Cathedral, where he built a central tower in 1343. He gave his house to Hythe as a hospital, later known as St Bartholomew's.

A mile inland **Saltwood Castle** was notorious as the overnight haven for the murderers of Becket on their way from France to Canterbury; latterly famous as the home of the art historian, the late Lord Clark. It is not open to the public, but the keep that comprises the modern home and the impressively extensive curtain walls can be seen from a public bridleway. In complete contrast, three miles or so to the west is Folkestone Racecourse – 8 miles from Folkestone. About 100 years old it is now, since the sudden demise of Wye some years ago, the only racecourse in the county. It suffered a bad period on the early 1960s with falling attendances and poor quality runners but a well organised appeal by Kent racegoers led to its reprieve. It is a friendly little course and, although the quality of runners at both flat and

Silting

Romney Marsh's status has always been ambivalent: sea or land? It has changed between the two several times since Neolithic times. When the Romans arrived, it was sea, but possibly it was beginning to silt up even then, as the open sea washed in shingle, and the shingle-built barriers then allowed alluvial silt to build up behind them. The great storm of 1287 that diverted the Rother changed Romney's status from proud Cinque Port to quiet inland town. Nemesis was awaiting Winchelsea, Rye, Lympne, and Hythe as well, not to mention Sandwich to the east, where different currents produced similar results, and where Queen Elizabeth's pragmatic refusal to give a grant of £10,000 for dredging sealed Sandwich's fate for good and all. As the alluvial level rose in the Romney area, in the 12th century farmers began to help the process by digging ditches and piling up walls of shale artificially: the Rhee Wall carrying the Appledore to Old Romney road above the marsh level is one such dyke. When Archbishop Becket saw the success of some of the small-scale operations, he set afoot a major reclamation project, and it may be that this in turn, by changing the pattern and thrust of the sea's currents, completed the combined natural and artificial reclamation of Romney and made it the richest grazing land in England.

Battle of Britain
When France collapsed before the might of Germany in 1940, and the British Expeditionary Forces had to be extricated in small boats from Dunkirk, Hitler remarked to General Jodl: 'The British have lost the war but they don't know it. Give them time and they will come round'. Goering intended to help the British to come round. He sent the *Luftwaffe* to soften up the defences of the realm, and to do that he had first to reduce the air defences of Kent. These consisted primarily of the Spitfire squadrons of 11 Group, RAF. They were based at Biggin Hill, West Malling, Detling, Eastchurch (in Sheppey), Manston, Hawkinge and Lympne. *Adlerangriff*, Eagle Attack, was how Goering proposed to win the battle of the air and prepare the way for Operation Sea-lion, the invasion of Britain. The German bombers flew in, accompanied by short-range Messerschmidt fighters to defend them. From 24 August until 6 September they concentrated on the south-eastern airfields, then, crucially and mistakenly, on London until on 15 September – Battle of Britain Day – the *Luftwaffe* threw everything they had into the air. They finished second best to the 'big wing' of Spitfires and Hurricanes led by Douglas Bader. Sea-lion was called off. The Battle of Britain had turned the war Britain's way. Today Manston and Hawkinge are air museums.

national hunt meetings is rarely high, the crowds have returned – to the discomfort of the goldfish in the paddock fish-pond who have had to become accustomed to visits from happy punters.

Stone-in-Oxney stands proud on the heights of the Isle of Oxney. Inside the church is a Roman altar to the god Mithras, very worn but with a carved relief of a bull still faintly discernible. Next door to the church is a lovely house of brick, tile and timber.

Snargate is a hamlet on the Rhee Wall, and has never been much bigger. It reduced William Cobbett to printed apoplexy. '. . . a village with *five houses*, and with a church capable of containing *two thousand people*! The *vagabonds* [Cobbett's favourite term of abuse for the government] tell us, however, that we have a *wonderful increase of population*! These *vagabonds* will be *hanged* by-and-by, or else justice will have fled from the face of the earth'.

Down a lane to the east, you cross to **Fairfield** from the road lost in a marshy wilderness south-west of Appledore along a grassy dyke. This is the place to find the essence of Romney Marsh. Anglers. Sea birds. Sheep grazing at the church door. Water is everywhere, sometimes even in the church which is the only building – there is no village, a fact which has given rise to many legends. If you go in May or June, the sound of marsh frogs will add its peculiar quality to the place: the males give a laughing call in the mating season. These are big frogs – they can eat mice. They were only introduced in 1934, when a few were tipped in a pond because they weren't needed for experiments, but they have spread since, to become as treasured a part of the scenery as the sheep and the birds. The church is dedicated to Thomas Becket, and the key is kept at Becket's Barn Farm (the only one in sight). Inside, it is magical. It was taken apart and lovingly put back together again by

WD Caroe in 1913, using as many of the original massive timbers as he could salvage. They straddle the nave and tiny chancel at not much more than head height. The nave is full of white box pews which turn uninterrupted into a pulpit with brass candlestick attached; there is a plain, honest font, and pews, the pulpit, and text boards are 18th century.

Brookland was where the smugglers called the Aldington Gang fought a bloody battle with the Excise men in 1821. Fights were not unusual – one of the houses in the village, Pear Tree Cottage, was the home of a doctor who was regularly taken blindfolded to tend wounded gang members. He always carried a medicine bag in case he was needed at short notice for such occasions. The church has a wooden belfry standing clear and shaped like a child's drawing of a Christmas tree. The spire fell off the church, the locals firmly hold, because of shock when a virgin came to be married. Inside is one of the most fascinating fonts in Christendom: Romanesque and lead, it shows the signs of the zodiac with reliefs of peasants at their labour: haymaking, threshing, treading grapes, collecting acorns. A 15th-century wall painting shows the murder of Becket.

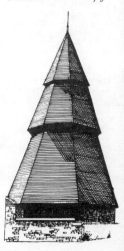

Brookland's wooden belfry

In the maze of the minor roads around Brookland, you can walk for hours without meeting traffic.

Brenzett inspired Kipling to write

Oh, Romney Level and Brenzett reeds,
I reckon you know what my mind needs.

William Cobbett found the village's remoteness less appealing: he complains in his *Rural Rides* that it was impossible to get a decent breakfast there.

John Fagge, father, and John Fagge, son, Cromwellians both, are commemorated in alabaster effigies in the church: one thing most of the churches have in common hereabouts is great hectoring puritanical text-boards on the walls or ceilings, and the 10 commandments inscribed in letters of gold on the reredos. This one sits bowered among tall trees in the tiny hamlet on the Rhee Wall.

Both Old and New Romney are very old indeed – they were well established before the Norman Conquest. **Old Romney** had three fisheries, a mill and a church at the time of Domesday. Now only the last is left, crouching on its haunches like a marsh frog, the steeply pitched nave roof almost as tall as the shingled spire. The floors are made of big red bricks, and the walls of white plaster, and there are box pews and a gallery. After the deluge of 1287, the villagers of **New Romney** broke their backs digging afresh the channel alongside the Rhee Wall, to try to coax the Rother back. All to no avail. The days of Cinque Port prosperity were gone. Today the little town is the headquarters of the **Romney, Hythe and Dymchurch Railway**, which runs through on its way between Hythe and Dungeness Lighthouse. It was conceived by two enthusiasts, whose whim of building a small-gauge public railway coincided with Southern Railway's plans at the time.

The first big victory of the Society for the Preservation of Ancient Buildings, founded by William Morris, was won at New Romney when it prevented a heavy-handed restoration of St Nicholas Church, which still has box pews. More recently the parish council insured the church for up to one million pounds. Storm damage was not covered, whereupon the storm of 1987 stripped the roof. The parishioners are working heroically to restore the church.

The pleasant High Street is in the Kentish tradition; but the best of the buildings is on the narrow road to Ivychurch where the stone wall of the two-storey remainder of the medieval St John's Priory overlooks the street with some eroded but lovely sculpted heads.

Lydd was the starting point for Pluto, the 'pipe-line under the ocean' built to supply the Allied Forces in Europe during World War II. It is said to have leaked and drenched the beaches with petrol, but the people of Lydd no doubt took satisfaction in the contribution to the war effort: the chancel of All Saints, Lydd had been flattened by a bomb in 1940, but not the tall tower with its fine Perpendicular vault. Cardinal Wolsey cut his teeth here as a vicar. Rubble walls in the north-west corner are the remains of the Saxon church and have been dated as early as the 5th century. The High Street west from the church is full of fine brick and stucco houses.

Ivychurch is where a clergyman was told that his service had been cancelled because the 'pulpit be full o' baccy, and vestry be full o' brandy'. There is a curious wooden structure like a sentry box (another one is at Brookland), but called a hudd and designed to shelter the parson from the Marsh rain during funerals.

The Buildings of England observes that St Rumwold, **Bonnington**, 'sits like a plump grey hen by the bank of the Royal Military Canal'. Exactly. This little building has a weatherboarded turret with an ogee-shaped lead cap and fluffed out flint base. A handsome slate slab in the churchyard marks the grave of the economist Lord Vaizey. Various tales of St Rumwold are told in Alan Bignell's *Kent Village Book*. One story is that he preached a sermon when he was two days old and died the day after; another is told in the *Ingoldsby Legends*, and has him reproving a bridegroom for swearing and eventually spiriting away his wife. Nearby **Bilsington** has a strange, ragged, weather-eaten obelisk in memory of Sir William Cosway, MP for Kent, who fell fatally from a stagecoach in the village in 1835. Edith M Nesbit, the author of *The Railway Children*, came to **St Mary-in-the-Marsh** as an old

Gavelkind
Like Devon and Cornwall, Kent's system of enclosed fields seems to have survived unscathed from the days of the Celtic and Belgic British tribes who lived here before the invasion of the Emperor Claudius. Unlike anywhere else in the British Isles, 'gavelkind' was law until 1925 in Kent. Gavelkind primarily provides for equal inheritance of land among all the sons of a father, and all inheritance is assumed to be by gavelkind unless it can be proved to have been provided for differently (whereas in other counties all inheritance was assumed to be by primogeniture). But gavelkind is more than this, it is a whole system of law, including accumulations of Roman statute providing for the womenfolk. The name is Saxon, from *gafol*, meaning rent. It implies a culture in which payment of rent to the lord in kind or cash was the norm rather than labour dues. Gavelkind applied only to the class of freemen which became known as yeomen. Consequently, large estates like Knole remained large; small holdings fragmented and became even smaller, though trading off between sons and finally increasing resort to Parliament kept landholdings to a viable size.

woman to live and to die here in 1924. A memorial plaque in the church has the epitaph: 'I will live among my children'.

The resort of **Dymchurch** is best known today as part of the name of the Romney, Hythe and Dymchurch Railway, but in the Middle Ages the Lords of Romney Marsh held court there. It was their responsibility to maintain the dykes which kept out the sea, in return for special privileges. It was also the scene of the 'Dymchurch Flit', described in Kipling's *Puck of Pook's Hill*, when England's last fairies took ship to France. There is a Martello tower, which can be visited.

An irrigation channel acts as a little moat to the most easterly of the Marsh churches, **Burmarsh**. Across the drawbridge and inside the porch is the best thing in the church: a Norman doorway with a manic head with ferociously bared teeth. In the little nave is a characteristic board with a text from Galatians perhaps for those who have been walking the marsh under one of its biting winds: 'Let us not be weary in well-doing: for in due season we shall reap, if we faint not'.

FURTHER READING

M. Baldwin,
The River and the Downs,
Gollancz, 1984

H. Belloc,
The Old Road,
London, 1904

A. Bignell,
The Kent Village Book,
Countryside Books, 1986

Gaius Julius Caesar,
The Conquest of Gaul,
Penguin, 1951

R. Church,
Kent, 1948,
Robert Hale, 1986

W. Cobbett,
Rural Rides,
Penguin, 1967

D. Defoe,
A Tour of England and Wales,
Everyman, 1927

F. Godwin and R. Ingrams,
Romney Marsh,
Wildwood House, 1980

F.W. Jessup,
A History of Kent,
Phillimore, 1974

W. Lambarde,
A Perambulation of Kent,
Chatham, 1826

J. Newman,
*The Buildings of England: North Kent
and the Weald,* and *North-East and
East Kent,*
Penguin, 1969

N. Nicolson,
Kent,
Weidenfeld and Nicholson, 1988

K. Spence,
*The Companion Guide to Kent and
Sussex,*
Collins, 1978

M. Waugh,
*Smuggling in Kent and Sussex
1700–1840,*
Countryside Books, 1985

C.J. Wright,
*A Guide to the Pilgrims' Way and the
North Downs Way,*
Constable, 1971

C. Wright,
Kent through the Years,
Batsford, 1975

*The Victoria History of the English
Counties: Kent* (in three volumes),
1908, 1926, 1932

Some of the above may be out of
print but should still be available
from libraries.